U-Turn Leadership

Lessons Learned from a Lifetime of Leadership

Elmer D. Gates

as told to
Peggy Salvatore

BALBOA.
PRESS
A DIVISION OF HAY HOUSE

Balboa Press books may be ordered through
booksellers or by contacting:

Balboa Press
A Division of Hay House
1663 Liberty Drive
Bloomington, IN 47403
www.balboapress.com
1 (877) 407-4847

Because of the dynamic nature of the Internet, any web addresses or
links contained in this book may have changed since publication and
may no longer be valid. The views expressed in this work are solely those
of the author and do not necessarily reflect the views of the publisher,
and the publisher hereby disclaims any responsibility for them.

The author of this book does not dispense medical advice or prescribe
the use of any technique as a form of treatment for physical, emotional,
or medical problems without the advice of a physician, either directly
or indirectly. The intent of the author is only to offer information
of a general nature to help you in your quest for emotional and
spiritual well-being. In the event you use any of the information in
this book for yourself, which is your constitutional right, the author
and the publisher assume no responsibility for your actions.

Any people depicted in stock imagery provided by Thinkstock are
models, and such images are being used for illustrative purposes only.
Certain stock imagery © Thinkstock.

Print information available on the last page.

ISBN: 978-1-5043-3881-3 (sc)
ISBN: 978-1-5043-3883-7 (hc)
ISBN: 978-1-5043-3882-0 (e)

Library of Congress Control Number: 2015913228

Balboa Press rev. date: 08/27/2015

Contents

To my wife, Betty, who managed the family while I was working, traveling, and learning my trade and, since her death, to my daughters, Patti and Jodi, who have cared for me and given me the time and encouragement to write this book

And to all leaders who Defy Convention

Acknowledgments

To Anne Baum, for helping me sharpen my focus on leadership by inviting me to be part of her Leadership Seminars and to partner with her in teaching an MBA leadership class.

To Teri Haddad D. Ed., for her encouragement to "stop talking and start writing." And I did.

To Peggy Salvatore, who was able to convert bullet points into the words you will read in this book.

If you run your business every day like you are in a turnaround situation, you'll never be in a turnaround situation.-Elmer D. Gates

Foreword

Results count!

To get results, you need a plan. More importantly, those plans need to be executed in order to have any value.

Plans are essential, but execution makes the world go 'round. Equal emphasis must be placed on both. Leadership is more than theory. That is why I am happy that Elmer has put his years of experience in this book so students can hear directly from him what execution looks and sounds like.

In *U-Turn Leadership*, Elmer introduces this essential principle: reject the status quo. At Clarkson University, that principle is expressed by our motto: Defy Convention.

The mind-set of rejecting the status quo—in other words, defying convention—is at the heart of fixing failing businesses and improving the performance of high-performing companies. In fact, the same principle informs start-up companies to prevent mistakes from being made at the outset. It is the fresh perspective that allows leaders to see clearly, unclouded by preconceived ideas and a "that's the way we've always done it here" mentality.

Success in the long term requires that these U-turn leadership principles be ingrained in the corporate culture.

Most importantly, the message for up-and-coming leaders is that you don't have to be a CEO to affect a turnaround. You can lead in your own functional unit, where you think like a CEO. After all, as Elmer says, you are the CEO of your assigned responsibilities. Act like it!

In this competitive and rapidly evolving global business environment, the only path to success is to Defy Convention because the conventional is passé. With responsibility pushed out farther to edges of the organization, it is incumbent upon developing leaders to assume responsibility for their own spheres of influence. Because great leadership is dependent on action, at Clarkson, we teach students how to decide and how to take action. We prepare our students to leave the world of theory for the world of application so that they can lead wherever they land.

Elmer's book is a light on the path of aspiring leaders as a how-to guide so that they can take effective action from day one in their areas of responsibility.

In all things, we encourage our students to take Elmer's advice: reject the status quo.

To the readers of *U-Turn Leadership*: I say Defy Convention!

Dr. Anthony G. Collins
President, Clarkson University

April 4, 2015

Introduction

A logical question to ask when reading a book on turnaround leadership is, "What causes a company to get to a point that it needs fixing?" The simple answer: failed leadership.

But I believe there is a much broader issue present in the majority of American companies, although I will add parenthetically that you will find this issue in corporations around the globe. In fact, too many corporate cultures are shaped by events rather than by the leader's vision of the organization. The culture in too many companies is one of maintaining the status quo. From the way the culture encourages stability to the way they write job descriptions, companies on a downward spiral are complacent at best and negligent at worst.

No matter the reason—complacency or outright negligence—nothing short of a culture shock can end the stagnation, and culture comes from the top. Leaders set the tone whether by design or default, which is simply by letting events shape the culture. I propose that great leaders lead by design; leadership by default is the broad highway to failure.

The problem with leadership doesn't start with the CEO. The board of directors bears a share of the responsibility by not probing, questioning, or disagreeing when things are amiss. A disengaged board gives rise to a discussion about the job of selecting directors and installing a system to regularly evaluate individual directors and the board as a whole. While the board cannot escape unscathed in this discussion, the focus of this book will be on the executive leadership, with an emphasis on the executive function—that is, the function to execute daily actions and decisions to steer the business to profitability.

Talking about turnaround leadership implies that you are a leader. Throughout this book, you will find tips to sharpen your leadership skills.

Why would a leader want to be involved in a turnaround? After all, leading a turnaround means assuming responsibility for a failing business. The material rewards of successful turnarounds are well known. Lesser publicized are the professional-development rewards for those leading the turnaround and for those leaders within the organization who survive the turnaround exercise. Successful U-turn leaders get their psychic income from the substantial improvement in operating results that are the outcome of their efforts. They have a chance to hone their unique leadership styles while instilling a culture of excellence.

The essence of executing a turnaround in an organization is to quickly determine the prevailing culture and destroy it ASAP. That is the easy part! The real work begins when you start building and maintaining the culture necessary to modify behaviors to create and sustain a high-performing organization.

In my turnaround successes and in leading successful businesses, I used a simple model that can be reduced to this formula:

- Focus intensely on the customer.
- Emphasize quality in all you do.
- Never make a commitment you don't intend to keep.

In too many of my turnaround experiences, there was no meaningful connection between the work being done by the employees and its value to the customer. Without that connection, an organization's people do not have a sense of the importance of their job. Disconnected employees lack the urgency to meet all their commitments to the customer in order to deliver a quality product on schedule. I usually found a lack of focus on quality in many of the important business functions as well.

Specifically, failing organizations lack quality in these areas:

- timely communication
- the content and format of communication
- the treatment of visitors and customers/outsiders
- communication and interaction with employees in and across functions (functional silos)

Each turnaround has its own unique cultural elements, but the above quality problems are almost surely present in every situation. Because most businesses in a turnaround situation evolved by default rather than deliberate decisions, practices can be destroyed in a very short time, so these shortcomings can be eliminated rather quickly.

The real work begins when you start to build the new culture.

In starting to build a better culture, determine your vision, mission, and long- and short-term goals. Then your first task is to define the desired outcome based on the vision, mission, and short- and long-term goals of the business. You should also set your expectations for each employee accordingly.

Once you are satisfied that you have defined the culture you intend to build, it's important that you communicate it to the entire organization. This cannot be a once-and-done written or verbal communication, although both delivery methods should be employed. It can't be done simply by hanging motivational posters. Verbal communication of the culture must be done in one-on-one conversations, in small meetings with targeted groups, and in large meetings with messages tailored to the total organization. Repetition is important.

As you make changes to the organization, you need to reinforce the initial communication with every action you take, every decision you make, and every communication you release at any level of the organization. In other words, you need to set the tone and lead by a consistently powerful and impactful example.

In the early days of your turnaround assignment, you will be making many tough decisions, which will create tension, fear, and some hostility. Don't buckle or cave in. You must continue to set the tone that things have changed. In this environment, as change is starting to happen, you will have to start earning respect and building mutual trust. Both are difficult to do simultaneously, but both are essential for the success of the turnaround.

In these following pages, I invite you to join me as I describe how I took stagnant enterprises and created cultures of massive engagement using these principles of U-turn Leadership – and how you can do it by design too, no matter where you are in the corporate hierarchy.

Part 1

Foundational Lessons

Part 1: Foundational Lessons

Boyhood

My generation was born into the Great Depression of the 1930s. We came of age with World War II, which took our older brothers and neighborhood buddies out of our towns and off our farms to fight a war against tyranny.

I don't think I am any different than the other men who grew up during this time. It was the time itself that was different and shaped our characters. Our experiences of poverty, solidarity, sacrifice, and promise made us different than the people who came before us and came after us. All generations have their unique environment, and that was mine.

My own boyhood was unexceptional for the time and place I grew up. We didn't have plumbing or electricity. I had a gun and used it to hunt for food. We didn't waste a lot of bullets on target practice; when we got a shot, it had to count because having meat to eat depended on it. We got to be good shots because we needed to be good shots.

During my college summers, I worked at a marina in the Adirondack Mountains in New York state. Many local college kids and young people from New York worked in the resorts. During the summer, young minorities from New York City, mostly African-Americans, would come up to the resorts to work in the hotels. One summer, a boatload of summer workers from New York City, enjoying their day off, rowed out into the lake and tipped over. Not all city kids can swim, and one was in danger of drowning. I drove a powerboat out to where their boat had capsized. I helped all but one up into the boat. He was drowning, and I was able to save him.

Since I was a resort worker and not a guest, I was limited to entering only the kitchen at the hotel where they worked as cooks and dishwashers. After the boating mishap that summer, whenever I visited the hotel kitchen, I could have anything I wanted on the menu, dessert included. What a treat for a struggling college kid!

My personal boyhood was not exceptional for that time, as previously mentioned. But compared to the world we live in today, my generation lived in an exceptional time.

Did it color the way I handled my responsibilities when I was called to lead? Most certainly.

After all, who we are—our upbringing, our gender, our age, our education, and our ethnicity—all contribute to the types of leaders we become. I address this in some detail in my course on leadership, accounting for different styles and recommending adaptations.

To sum it up, your personal leadership style is unique to you. There is no right or wrong personal style, only differences among people. Just as in all other areas of your life, don't try to copy another person's leadership style. It won't work. Refine your own style.

Your own leadership style is molded by

- your ethnicity;
- your gender;
- your upbringing;
- your education; and
- your life's experiences.

There is a spectrum of behaviors within each category. Generally, however, you will find that these five qualities influence the way you lead. For example, usually women are better at building relationships than men. However, the same person who is strong at relationship building may have more trouble dealing with difficult decisions involving people. So while women tend to be better at relationships, men tend to be better at making difficult personnel decisions. Women are also better at multitasking than men, and women are better with details than men.

A person who worked throughout high school and college will have learned a lot about leading by watching the leaders they worked for. They will also understand accountability and two-way communication. A person without this experience will have to learn these skills upon entering the workforce.

For the purposes of this book, to perhaps help the reader understand the type of leadership that was comfortable for me, it may help to explain that I am the product of my environment—a time, place, and way of life that isn't all that common today.

I was able to learn these lessons on my own, with help from great parents and a lot of role models and leaders who guided me along my career. And I share them here with you so that you might find some guidance as you travel your own leadership path.

Chapter 1

A Young Lieutenant and a Bridge

You can improve any situation you inherit, and when you know you are right, have confidence. The measured risk you take will have a payoff.

Wartime creates an environment where you either learn quickly or too late. I learned that lesson, like most military men, under pressure.

I did not realize until years later that not all the lessons that shaped my philosophy about business were lessons in turnarounds. In truth, all of my experiences, from the time I left my boyhood home in New York state to when I was walking the barren landscape of Korea, laid the foundation that shaped my leadership style and my career.

After all, each of us develops a leadership style from the time we come to the age of realization. We do this in family situations as an older brother or sister, in the classroom when volunteering to deliver things to the office or serving as class president, and on the playground as the captain of the neighborhood baseball team. We also learn how to become de facto leaders, the unappointed and unelected leaders of our peer groups, by deciding which game to play or which ice cream shop to visit.

Most of us don't realize the myriad of leadership experiences we have growing up and how those experiences develop our personal leadership styles. As we grow into mature leaders, we do well to reach back into those foundational lessons to become the unique leaders we are meant to be.

Our job in becoming great leaders is not to imitate someone else's leadership style, but rather to continue to refine our own personal leadership style—the one that evolved from the first time your peer group attended the movie *you* wanted to see.

⠿

My first exposure to a turnaround occurred in 1952 during the Korean War. I had landed my first paid leadership assignment when I was a twenty-two-year-old combat engineering platoon leader in Korea. It wasn't a turnaround as we experience them in organizations today, but it taught me a valuable lesson and a set of skills I utilized in turnarounds for the rest of my career. That lesson? Any situation can be improved; therefore, the status quo is not acceptable. But I didn't realize what I had learned at the time: reject the status quo.

In Korea, I was expected to perform in the moment, assessing situations and responding, then monitoring results and adjusting on the fly. It wasn't a situation that allowed time for reflection. However, when I returned to work in industry and saw how the lessons I learned in Korea applied in every situation I encountered in the private sector, this essential truth sank in.

Any situation can be improved. Reject the status quo.

My platoon of approximately twenty soldiers was assigned to the 5th Marine Regiment. Our job was to clear minefields, build bridges, and tend a floating (Widgeon) bridge over the Imjim River close to the west coast of Korea. The Imjim River was close enough to the ocean that the tides affected the height of the river. We had to adjust the bridge over the Imjim River twice a day to accommodate the changing tides to supply the front lines and bring back the wounded, the POWs, and more. The bridge not only required an adjustment to compensate for tidal action, but the challenge was compounded by the fact that Korea is a country with steep mountains and little mature vegetation, which exacerbated flooding after the heavy rains during the rainy season. In theory, the bridge could be disassembled when the floods came.

The first day after I arrived, I went down to the bridge to understand what I had inherited. I was struck by the many pieces of the bridge—the large number of rubber pontoons and steel treads—that had washed down river from the bridge site.

When I looked down the length of the river and saw all those parts, it bothered me. "What happened down there?"

The guys told me, "We just can't get this bridge pulled in time when the floods come. We don't have enough time to get the bridge disassembled."

I thought it was an interesting problem. The design of the bridge utilized large rubber pneumatic pontoons in which the air pressure enabled the surface of the bridge to float. Steel treads were mounted on the pontoon floats, and vehicles were able to drive on the treads. The design seemed sufficient to the task, but clearly the assembly and disassembly presented a persistent problem in this unique circumstance.

In retrospect, this situation led me to make the only decision of my career that required me to use my mechanical engineering degree.

After a week or so of getting familiar with my fellow platoon members, building a bridge a few miles upriver, and getting reports on tidal action as well as learning about the bridges, I started studying the construction of this particular bridge. The steel treads, which comprised the driving surface of the bridge, were connected from one pontoon to the next by two steel rods, both two and a half inches in diameter and three feet long, driven through holes in each end of the treads.

When the flood waters came, the water would distort the bridge into an arc, thereby stressing every connection point and making it impossible to remove the pins.

After understanding the connecting mechanism and watching differently sized vehicles travel over the bridge, I realized that by modifying two of the treads in the middle of the bridge, we could prevent the loss of any more bridge parts during the flooding if we could reduce the time it took to disconnect the treads. All that was required was to convert the two holes into slots in one end of the two treads in the middle of the bridge.

I had our welder burn the metal below the hole in the tread to make the slot. The slot made it possible to use the lift on one of our bridge trucks to pull the treads up and out of the slots and then fold them back on the treads behind them. The bridge was then in two pieces, and the winches on our bridge trucks, positioned on each side of the river, could hold the bridge halves on the shore until the flood receded. When the water had subsided, our boats pulled the two halves of the bridge back into position. We lowered the two treads to connect the two halves, and the bridge was completely ready to be traversed again. This new arrangement cut just enough time off disassembly to make it possible to pull the two halves of the bridge before the flooding came.

The bridge modification was not without its trouble. Our welder had a cracked, smoked glass window in his welding helmet and was temporarily blinded by the work done on the modification. That meant that in addition to using my mechanical engineering degree skills, I also learned some basic welding skills. The weld wasn't pretty, but in the end, it worked.

Finally, the modification was tested under pressure.

We had a severe rain, and the order came down from the commanding officer for everybody to pull their bridges. I said, "No, sir. I am not going to do it."

That prompted a visit from the group operations officer. We knew each other. He had been my company commander before his promotion to his current position.

He repeated his order. "Gates, pull that bridge."

"No, sir," I said as respectfully, but as firmly, as I could muster. I hadn't told him about the fix to the bridge. I said, "No way. I know this river a hell of a lot better than you do, and I don't need to pull it."

"Do you know what you are doing?" he demanded of me.

I said I knew. "Yes, sir. I am violating the direct order of a superior officer."

"Okay," he said, satisfied that I understood the consequences of my refusal.

That night, despite the order, my bridge stayed in place, although it was nip and tuck whether we should pull it. However, I knew that at the very last minute, we could use my adaptation and pull it. So we held out, the bridge remained intact, and I took back all the wounded, prisoners of war, and all the rocket launchers that, in the Korean War, were towed by Jeeps. The bridge held.

The next morning, a helicopter flew into the Marine bivouac area right next to our position. A brigadier general emerged and asked, "Who's in charge of the bridge?" The Marines damn well knew who that was. They sent for me.

I drove up in my jeep. A soldier stood by the helicopter, and he had a star on his helmet, so I knew he was a brigadier general. I saluted.

"Lieutenant Gates reporting, sir."

He returned the salute, eyed this young upstart, and asked, "Were you in charge of this bridge last night?"

"Yes, sir."

"I just want to shake your hand. You kept your head when a lot of guys lost it last night," the brigadier general said to me.

"Thank you, sir," I said, then turned on my heel and left.

For a twenty-two-year-old, newly promoted first lieutenant, that was pretty heady stuff!

There is another facet to this story that contained some lessons of its own. Sometime later, our combat engineering group commander, a lieutenant colonel, received the Army Commendation Medal for the improvement I made for this type of bridge.

My reward came later.

I learned that when you are confident and know the facts, you need to make a measured decision and stick with it. The improvement in the bridge connection was a big factor in my decision to disobey the order to pull the bridge. I knew the bridge, I knew the river, and I knew the risk. In other words, I was knowledgeable in my area of responsibility.

Another lesson is embedded in this experience too. When you work for someone else, your boss often gets the credit. Employees are there to make their bosses successful, and bosses are charged with making their employees successful. The situation of reciprocal, mutual responsibilities between the boss and employees is the key to long-term success. This important lesson stayed with me. Leaders and employees have a mutual responsibility to make each other successful.

I learned that if employees do well, they will get their turn at the helm. I encountered plenty of examples of that later in my career as well.

While it took a few years to realize the lessons I learned by this experience, my subsequent leadership roles confirmed everything I discovered as a twenty-two-year-old lieutenant assigned to the bridge over the Imjim River: reject the status quo.

Chapter 1: Takeaways

1. Reject the status quo.
2. Look beyond the obvious.
3. Be decisive and then take action.
4. Take measured risks.
5. Know the important details of your responsibilities.

Chapter 2

Management Style Emerges at General Electric

You don't have to be a CEO to improve the performance of your company. You just have to think like a CEO.

General Electric is one of the corporations that defined twentieth-century post-WWII America. During the 1950s, when the US buzzed with big cars, jets, and jukeboxes, the head of the Screen Actors Guild, Ronald Reagan, was GE's spokesman. With its global reach and deep pockets, midcentury GE provided fertile ground for leadership opportunities.

But as a large corporation with multiple organizational levels, it was also a place where employees could be absorbed into the dense corporate fabric and quietly remain until retirement. This changed when Jack Welch became CEO.

For this confident, young Korean-War veteran, GE provided ample opportunities to exercise the lessons of strong leadership, thoughtful risk-taking, and applied engineering acquired at the expense of the US Army.

After my army service, I returned to GE in Syracuse, New York, and was assigned as facilities supervisor of a plant in Utica, New York, part of GE's Commercial and Government Equipment Department. I commuted every day from Syracuse to Utica by car.

We were housed in an old warehouse building. The offices inside were quite nice, but the parking lot had not been maintained. The lot was pockmarked with holes, it was rough, and it caused problems for employees and suppliers who drove over cracks and potholes in the deteriorating surface. The dividing lines were nonexistent, and it was an inconvenience at best and a hazard at worst. People groused loudly about the condition of the parking lot.

Since I was charged with facilities maintenance, I had to fix it. So I hired a company to pave it. Asphalt, then and now, is expensive. My boss came down and saw the newly paved parking lot.

"What happened here?"

"I paved the lot," I said.

"You don't have the money for that."

He was right. I didn't have it budgeted. It just needed to be done.

"Where are you going to get the money?" he asked.

"Don't worry about it. We'll get it," I assured him.

And we did.

What happened after the parking lot was paved? People were happier. They knew they were important. There was a significant change in attitude on the part of the employees, and our productivity improved. We were able to pay for resurfacing, even though the parking lot improvement was not originally planned. Other cost-saving decisions helped me meet our budget.

By this time, leadership lessons were starting to take shape. Based on my early experience in Korea, I knew I could rely on my knowledge of the situation and use my judgment to take a calculated risk. I learned to assume the authority to do what I thought was right.

The Utica experience led to my next leadership lesson: when you treat your employees right, listen to their complaints, and satisfy them when it is practical, you are going to have a much happier and more productive workforce.

> *Take care of your people.*

My next assignment was in Auburn, New York, where my group was charged with developing the process to manufacture printed circuit boards. The use of printed circuit boards in electronics was newly introduced. The original process required the company to buy large sheets of copper-clad, nonconductive laminate and print the circuit pattern on the copper. The next step required the copper to be etched away in an acid bath, leaving only the copper circuit pattern. Multiple circuit boards were printed on one piece of copper-clad laminate. After the acid bath left the circuit patterns, the sheets were rinsed, dried, and cut into individual circuit boards.

Because the process required us to etch away most of the copper, it resulted in a lot of copper loss. The design engineers were looking for a way to reduce the cost of this expensive process. If we could only pay for the copper we used and eliminate the cost of all the waste, we could save a lot of money. We spent the next two years working on a process to reduce the amount of copper waste.

We decided on a plan to buy bare laminate with no copper clad on it. We would spray an adhesive and a silver conductive surface and then print the negative circuit pattern on the silver surface using a silk-screen process. Finally, we would plate the copper onto the circuit pattern, rather than etch the copper off to expose the pattern. By using this silk-screen process, we thought we would not only save a lot of expensive copper, but we could also change the circuitry design more quickly.

We spent a lot of hours and a lot of money on the many steps leading to the silk-screen process. The idea seemed sound.

For my role, I traveled to visit suppliers of different materials and equipment. I visited companies that manufactured adhesives. We purchased conductive material to spray on the bare laminate. We had to purchase machinery to print the circuit design and to prepare the bare laminate.

Finally, for all our efforts, we could not overcome the technical challenges of plating the circuit. And even had the idea worked—which it did not—the new process would not have resulted in meaningful savings.

Technically and financially, we had to abandon the idea.

GE paid for this expensive lesson that I was able to add to my growing list of leadership lessons. I found that all my leadership lessons would not come from successes; some of the lessons would come from failures.

In this case, our bosses acknowledged our sincere efforts to improve the process and save the company money. Yes, we took a whole new approach, and we failed. Nobody got blamed, and nobody got fired. I saw a culture of innovation in action at GE and learned that all risk decisions aren't successful from a business perspective.

We failed for the right reasons. It wasn't practical to plate copper onto a nonconductive material. We simply said, "Well, there is another experiment."

Progress requires people to get out of their comfort zones, challenge the status quo, and be decisive. Being decisive includes knowing when to forge ahead, and it also includes knowing when all options are exhausted—that is, when to declare an experiment unsuccessful.

At GE, failure was tolerated, if for the right purpose. In the spirit of continual progress and improvement, the message to employees was, "Keep trying." No worthy idea was dismissed. Experimentation and innovation were encouraged. Random failure was one result.

A country and a world leapt forward during the twentieth century due to the kind of leadership that allows people to fail in the interest of research. These are lessons we want to preserve as we continue to make technological strides into an increasingly amazing future.

In fact, at GE, we were already part of what was then one of humanity's most amazing feats—the NASA program to put the first man in space. More about that experience follows.

NASA: Daytona Beach, a Government Contract, and a Few More Lessons

GE played an important role in the early days of America's space program. In the 1960s, America was focused on putting a man on the moon. The United States was locked in a competition with our Cold War adversary, the then-Soviet Union, to win that race. The 1960s was the decade of space travel, and many of our country's resources were dedicated to the effort.

GE built a major manufacturing and engineering facility in Daytona Beach, Florida, due to its proximity to Cape Canaveral, the location of the launching pads for the rockets that put the payloads into space. It was a multi-building complex built to serve one customer, the National Aeronautics and Space Administration.

After my exposure to several GE businesses in my early years with the company, I was assigned to Dayton Beach in 1962, a few days before the birth of my youngest daughter. I was part of the group that was responsible for building the ground support equipment to put the first American man into orbit around the earth, a necessary precursor to getting all the way to the moon.

My first position was manager of facilities. Later, I became the factory manager. GE held a government contract to build the ground support equipment used in the prelaunch and the very early stage of the launch. In this era, the launch vehicle was the Atlas Missile.

We were primarily an assembly shop. We had a diverse factory workforce, many people having the best job of their careers. I had an experienced production control manager who scheduled the factory, ensured the availability of materials, and just generally made sure we had the people and resources we needed on time. NASA employed auditors who oversaw our work.

Our factory workers started their shift at 7:00 a.m., and the office hours started an hour later, at 8:00 a.m. Most of us who worked in the offices arrived early for the 8:00 a.m. shift, usually at 7:15 or 7:30 a.m., as is customary in manufacturing. However, one morning, NASA auditors visited our site unannounced and stationed themselves at each door. They wrote a report saying that my office workers were late. Of course we were not late, but the inspectors didn't allow for two different start times. The federal auditors did not have the flexibility to understand or compensate for two different shift schedules. We explained the shift differential to no avail. Finally, in frustration, I told my office employees that if they saw the NASA guy standing around when they arrived, they should go back home and come in after 9:00 a.m. when they were gone.

"Then we'll be perfect," I reasoned.

It worked. The auditors refused to understand we had two starting times and did not check our procedure before conducting the audit. To avoid being written up, I had to work around them. My boss called me in to explain to him why we were written up for being late.

"You were here at seven thirty," he said, accusing us of missing our start time.

"It's easy to explain," I said. "Our starting time is eight o'clock, and we get here at seven thirty. What more do you need?"

He didn't question the office staff's starting time after that, and we understood that the government was more interested in their process than in the results we got. I had the courage to send people home to get better marks from NASA. A lot of guys would not have done that, but the bureaucracy didn't allow for practical adjustments to the rules.

At one point, we had six individual contracts and were late on all of them. The production control manager came into my office and gave me hell.

"Gates, you need to get tougher on the general foremen. You need to insist they give you a get-well plan to get back on schedule in a month," he said.

"I will," I promised.

I got the general foremen to give me schedules, held them accountable to stick to them, and we were mostly back on schedule in a month, as planned. The experience taught me that a commitment is just that. Excuses are unacceptable. That lesson made me a better leader. Results count; excuses don't!

The high-profile, high-pressure NASA contract gave me the opportunity to observe two types of bosses in action—the best and the worst. The two experiences resulted in valuable lessons since we learn from both types of leaders—one on purpose and one inadvertently.

The worst bosses I have observed cannot handle pressure. They get sick when things get really tough. Whenever there is a crisis, they abdicate responsibility and look to others for advice and support because they live in uncertainty. They call meetings and set up committees to avoid making a decision. From them, I learned that leaders who cannot make a decision or commit to a course of action simply are not leaders at all. They waste time and resources and don't know how to build a team.

In a high-profile situation like the NASA-manned space mission, incompetence is the exception. More competent and excellent people were involved in the project than not, which accounted for its success, of course.

During my four years in Florida, the chief project manager of the GE program stands out as one of the best leaders I have ever observed. He had an enormous amount of responsibility to oversee the pre-launch details, and he was singularly focused on them. I learned just how focused he was the day NASA sent our first astronaut, Alan Shepard, into space. Somebody, who the project manager did not particularly respect on our team, asked him, "Hey, how are they going to get him down?"

"I don't give a damn," he shot back. "Our job was to get him up there, and we did! It's someone else's job to get him down."

He once said of this fellow, "If he were to forecast failure, and it happened, he would feel he was a success."

In that one moment, that excellent project manager revealed his single-mindedness about his responsibilities. From his reaction, I learned that it is important to stay focused on what you are paid to do. If you involve yourself in your own responsibilities, you'll do a better job. And, just as importantly, that man demonstrated that a leader makes things happen. An administrator watches things happen.

We watched the launch because we made it happen.

Chapter 2: Takeaways

1. Take care of your people.
2. Focus on your own responsibilities.
3. Get out of your comfort zone.
4. Learn from your failures. Every failure is tuition.
5. Apologize. Don't ask, just do it. Take action!
6. Don't surrender to regulations or auditors.
7. Results count. Excuses don't.

Chapter 3

Balanced Production Program at General Electric's Erie Plant

Managers at every level don't understand the details of their business. They do not have a knowledge-based organization.

If you accept the philosophy of *reject the status quo*, then you understand that any organization can be improved. You can use the lessons in this book to affect the turnaround or improvement in a functional unit at any level of an organization or in a total business.

I started learning these lessons at a unit level early in my career and found that they apply wherever you find yourself within the organization. In fact, a single turnaround in one part of the business can have positive impact on other functional business units and a large, positive financial impact on the total business, as I found in my next experience at GE.

After several formative years based in Syracuse, New York, GE transferred me to Erie, Pennsylvania, where I traveled the professional development path set for me by the general manager. According to plan, GE promoted me through a series of managerial roles with ever greater responsibilities within the direct current motor and generator department—first as manager of manufacturing engineering, then as manager of employee relations, and finally to manager of manufacturing. GE's DCM&G was a very successful business.

In Erie, we were a typical job shop. We built various-sized motors that powered some of the processes of the big corporations that powered the global economy— companies like Boise Cascade, Ingersoll Rand, and Bucyrus Erie. If one of our motors failed or was delivered late, our customers sustained serious losses in productivity, efficiency, and ultimately revenue. The failure of a GE motor impacted the customers as well. We shouldered a lot of responsibility to these customers to deliver products that performed optimally in a timely fashion. When our motors were shipped late or didn't perform according to specifications, the customers would often seek reparations from GE for their losses.

During the Erie assignment, I gained credibility in a large organization, demonstrating that I could improve the situation and make a difference. When I went to Erie, there was no expectation put on me to make things better. That is not a criticism of GE; I just got hired because somebody left.

"Okay, Gates, fill these shoes."

This was my first experience of being hired into a position description that did not describe the job to be done. Rather, I was reissued an existing position description that had been written some time ago. The job description I filled did not take into account the issues in the business or what was required to perform optimally. I had to figure that out for myself. That experience helped me begin to realize position descriptions are usually inadequate. They describe the past.

Finding the Problems

By the time I got to Erie, I had the confidence to move ahead and make changes. I felt confident enough to make them on my own without having to get anybody to approve them. It was there that I really began to understand that you can make improvements at every level—in this case, manufacturing—and that there was a great opportunity to impact the whole business. Shortly after arriving, I found a problem of uneven production on the manufacturing line.

The problem of unbalanced production was a way of life. Everyone accepted the conventional wisdom that we were a job shop and that, by nature, job shops are inefficient. By rejecting the status quo, I was free to succeed or fail in my efforts to improve the situation with no oversight. Also, I figured that anything I did was a low-risk move since even if my program didn't work, we would be no worse off than when I arrived. So I was able to keep improving our processes with no interference until I got it right.

Elmer D. Gates

When I arrived, I found we were shipping a large percentage of our product during the last week of the month. Initially, I simply recognized that this practice was causing huge inefficiencies in my organization. It was not until later, when production improved, did I realize there would also be a positive effect on cash flow. Before the Balanced Production Program began, our cash flow was thirty days from the last week of every month, when most of our product was sent. By getting product shipped out each week through balancing the production on the manufacturing line, payments became due thirty days from each week's shipments, providing a more even cash flow. That Balanced Production Program was a turning point in my life, and because of that, greater expectations began to be placed on me after my work in Erie.

I started, though, by tackling the most obvious problems.

Since I had the benefit of working in manufacturing previously, I had a good idea of the kind of immediate changes that needed to be made. The first was housekeeping. Put simply, I had learned during my time in manufacturing engineering that the units with good housekeeping practices—those that were neat and tidy, with everything in its place—also had higher productivity and better quality output. So neatness was my priority. I knew that some problems could be solved with small but significant measures. I initiated a best housekeeping award and presented it monthly to the foreman with the neatest area.

I considered establishing a tail-end award for the messiest area but was talked out of it by less confrontational personalities than my own. At that point in my career, I felt that life was a win-lose situation. If you failed to win, you lost. There were no ties in my world. In retrospect, the decision not to create the tail-end award was the right one.

Labor Strife

Our factory workers at the GE Erie plant were members of the United Electrical, Radio and Machine Workers of America (UEW). The union had a colorful history, some of their leaders having been charged and convicted as communists in the 1950s during the developing Cold War. It was an active, and activist, union, and I came into management during these years. The union was powerful, bargaining not only with GE but also representing workers at other major American corporations, like Westinghouse Electric and RCA.

My confrontational style was evident in the way I handled many situations. For example, in several places throughout the factories, there were household-type refrigerators used to store various adhesives, epoxies, and other insulating materials used in production. During the process of cleaning up the shops, we discovered that employees were keeping their lunches and snacks in the shop refrigerators. This practice not only violated health-department regulations, but it defied common sense as well. I ordered more appropriate coolers for our supplies and placed them in restricted areas to the factory workers. This meant that employees no longer had a place to store their lunches. I made no friends with the workers for this decision.

When I replaced the refrigerators with dedicated coolers for manufacturing materials, the union put an ad in the local newspaper announcing "Free Refrigerators," which directed callers to my home phone number. I received a large number of phone calls late at night inquiring about the refrigerators.

Much of my time in Erie was punctuated with labor issues while instituting efficient management practices.

Several business units were housed in seven or eight buildings at the Erie plant. Labor contracts were negotiated on a plant-wide basis by a centralized office. At one point during my tenure there, we sustained a strike. Several weeks of negotiations broke down, an agreement could not be reached, and the union called a strike. Issues of work rules and pay were on the table. Union members of each business picketed at the appropriate gate to the plant, so we knew "our pickets." The pickets were aggressive, requiring police presence around the clock, but fortunately, there were no injuries.

However, my factory workers were not deterred by the police presence. Their first action was to get a truckload of horse manure dumped in my driveway at home. That was humorous, but then things got serious.

While we still had two young daughters at home, my life was threatened. We received a phone call at night that repeated the message. From that point forward, we had 24/7 security for the duration of the strike.

At the plant, union pickets held signs saying, "Up With Rates. Down With Gates" and "Hitler is Alive and Well in the Body of ED Gates." The strike lasted about six weeks.

There were folks in employee relations and senior management who were willing to concede some things, but I said no, we weren't going to concede. At that time, if there was a truce with the unions, that meant that we lost. I felt that if we gave in on anything, it was a loss. I didn't concede on work rules. However, I didn't have a final say on compensation, although I certainly was a champion not to meet their total demands. I measured the win in that we gave no concessions on work rules.

When an agreement was reached, I was told to "make nice" with the union. I set up a meeting in my office with union officials. Before the meeting, I had huge enlargements made of two pickets signs and hung them on my office wall so that they were facing them throughout the meeting.

"A contract has been reached. I will adhere to it, and I expect you to do the same," I began. "I will continue to improve this operation, and I hope you will help. Any questions?"

They had none.

"Thank you for meeting with me today. We have disappointed our customers by missing our delivery dates. We'll have to get to work to make up the time."

They did, and we continued implementing the Balanced Production Program.

Balanced Production Program at GE

Our operation was a job shop that produced small quantities of a variety of models of motors and generators, varying from production runs of one to ten motors at a time. After a few months of gaining familiarity with the operation, I identified some major inefficiencies.

As I mentioned earlier, we usually completed 60 to 70 percent of our billing in the last week of the month. Sometimes we would stretch the last weekend of the month into the next month in order to meet the schedule. This practice led to very costly amounts of overtime and significant shortages of parts that had been scavenged from motors further back in the assembly line.

> *Even if the company thinks all is well, there is room for improvement in every part of the business.*

When we came into the shop at the beginning of the next month, a parts shortage across the factory caused idle time everywhere. Idle time is inefficient and costly. Idle time in manufacturing is comparable to non-billable time for an attorney or an accountant; the clock was running, but we weren't manufacturing very much. We went from running in overdrive on the last day of the month to sitting in neutral during the first week of the month.

"For Chrissake, we can't continue to do this," I said.

The impacts of the unbalanced production schedule on operations were several, significant, and bad for the bottom line:

1. Tremendous amounts of overtime in both time-and-a-half and double-time were used in the last week and weekend of the month.
2. Quality suffered, resulting in warranty costs later. (I used the 1:5:25 rule to calculate the costs of manufacturing defects. For example, if you fix a

defect at the point a product is made, it costs one dollar to correct; if the defect is found later in the assembly line or during testing, packing, or shipping, it costs five dollars to fix it; and if the defect is discovered after the product leaves the factory, that same correction costs twenty-five dollars.)

3. Because parts were scavenged from all over the factory so that motors could be assembled and shipped before the month's end, we started every new month with parts shortages. This caused much idle time throughout the shop at the beginning of the month.

4. Cash flow was impaired negatively by late billing, and the quality problems caused by the inefficient utilization of the manufacturing process led to delayed payment or nonpayment by customers.

After mulling over a possible course of action, I set a goal of getting 25 percent of our output shipped each week to achieve consistent workflow and billing. I named the initiative the Balanced Production Program and involved all my direct reports:

- one manufacturing engineering manager
- one quality control manager
- one materials manager
  - purchasing
  - shipping
  - receiving

- three shop operations superintendents
  - general foremen
  - foremen

Defining the Problems

I called a meeting with my direct reports and announced that I would meet with them over lunch individually on a rotating basis for three days a week. At first, I thought I just had to bring in the guys[1] reporting to me. But they couldn't tell me what was causing the unbalanced production and didn't know the details of their organization, so I went one level down, looking for answers. I found the same situation. Finally, I went down to the foreman level, and at all three levels, the leaders didn't know the important details of processes, quality, schedules, material availability, and so forth. I couldn't believe it. We did not have a knowledge-driven organization.

As an example, I asked a coil-winding foreman, "What's your yield?"

He had no idea. He based everything on 100 percent yield and assumed he had all his parts and that there

---

[1] I use the terms "guys," "foremen," "salesmen," and other gender-specific pronouns because in the era in which I was in management at GE, the colleagues to whom I refer were men. If I refer to a secretary, it was a woman in those days. This is not to ignore the fact that this has changed, which will be reflected in my later experiences, but my intent is to give an authentic flavor of the time and an accurate accounting of the environment in which I worked.

were no defects among them. So if he encountered a problem, he said, "Whoops! We won't have that part on time." In his mind, overtime was the solution for this situation, whether a worker was absent or a machine had broken down. Overtime was every leader's best friend.

After the second round of meetings was complete, I confirmed that while the managers were good, they lacked in-depth knowledge of the work being done in the organization. I also realized if we were going to be dealing with facts, we needed to involve *their* direct reports in these meetings as well. That decision to go deep into the organization to get answers redefined the scope of the Balanced Production Program.

What started as a few investigational meetings became a three-year process with three meetings each week. At the end of the three years, it paid off. We achieved our goal of shipping 25 percent of the month's billing each week.

Over three years, I held box-lunch meetings three days a week, rotating the function. We had to dig down deeply into each functional area to get all the information we needed to figure out what exactly was happening. Each superintendent had three general foremen, and they, in turn, had three to five foremen working for them. The supporting functions all had a few supervisors working for them. We needed to get to the frontline supervisors to learn the facts about what was happening in each area of the shop. Changes had to be based on facts. It took many more meetings to get those facts and make the appropriate changes than I initially anticipated.

I was appalled at how little each level of the organization knew about what was really important and happening in every production unit, and frankly I was appalled by their lack of concern or their lack of embarrassment by it. I was also appalled at the lack of communication among the several functional areas. For example, the shop superintendents did not insist that their production control people check material availability for the next week or longer! The production and material areas operated independently of one another, even though their functions were mutually dependent.

> *Leaders at each level of the organization knew little about what was happening in their production unit.*

Specifically, I found that

- managers at every level of the organization did not know details of the important, if not the critical, operations and processes in their areas of responsibility, and they did not practice or insist on forward planning from their people;
- reports received by the managers reporting to me were primarily based on results, with no analysis or corrective action and no cross training. Since the business was doing fine, there was no sense of urgency to improve;

- a culture of complacency had taken hold in the organization. The business was making money. Life was good there, and nobody wanted to disturb it;

- there was no in-depth analysis of quality levels (yield rate of important processes) and no documentation of patterns of absenteeism, and so they believed that the only solution was overtime. There was no cross training. The supervisors did not check the availability of materials for the current and next week's production, and there was no analysis of the cause of idle time; and

- frontline foremen were selected on the basis of which employee was the best craftsman in the organization, with little concern for their management or leadership ability. After capable employees were promoted, no leadership training was provided.

I found some variation in the level of knowledge of people within different operations. At each level of management, there were deficiencies prevalent across the organization. Some of the variation included the percent of rejects in each process, the causes and possible fixes of problems, what changes would improve the yield, the availability of materials for each week's production, no plan to cover absenteeism, no cross training, and no requests for studies by quality control or manufacturing engineering to address these variations.

The supervisors and foremen never had a plan to provide for absenteeism. If a man was absent, somebody would work overtime rather than having another employee cross-trained to fill the gap.

"Well, that won't work," I told them. "You have to do some cross-training." By cross-training our workforce, we were building a more knowledgeable and flexible workforce.

Change has to come from the top, and since during the discovery phase I found problems at every level, I knew solutions had to be implemented at every level too. It would have to start with direction from me.

Management reports were superficial due to a lack of depth in understanding the capability of the operations in areas of responsibilities. These deficiencies presented me with opportunities to teach the following:

1. Know the yield of every process. If you see deterioration in the process, determine if it is a machine problem or an operator problem. Then take corrective action.
2. Determine the availability of parts for the month's output and factor in yield when determining quantities. If there are shortfalls, take corrective action.
3. Plot attendance patterns over the long term and develop and implement cross-training programs as appropriate to eliminate or minimize the necessity for overtime.

4. Measure productivity and determine the factors impacting it (machine capability, quality levels, absenteeism, parts availability, etc.). Take appropriate action to repair, maintain, or improve the situation.

The expectations laid out to the managers at all levels of the organization required them to communicate extensively with other functions. In this way, silos were reduced or eliminated, leading to a more knowledgeable and responsive team.

Prior to the implementation of the Balanced Production Program, none of these considerations were included in managers' plans. After these disciplines were built into the culture of the organization, the improvements continued for quite some time. However, I found that if all of these important factors were not managed closely, poorer performance would gradually return. One overarching lesson I have learned is this: In any organization, there is always a tendency to want to relax when things start to go well. It's the leader's job to constantly outline new challenges for the organization in order to prevent this from happening.

The above lessons apply to a manufacturing business, but these factors apply to any successful business. Set expectations, make sure every level of management knows what is expected, and then manage the critical success factors. Build a knowledge-based organization.

Despite all the problems I uncovered, when I arrived in Erie, things had been going well to the casual observer. The department had become satisfied with the status quo. I learned a great deal from this experience; it opened my eyes to the huge opportunities for every business to improve.

Results Oriented

After three years of three luncheon meetings per week, productivity improved. Cash flow improved too. After we implemented changes, we had productivity in the plant during the first day of the month. Plus, we had a much more knowledgeable and aware leadership team, from my direct report down to the foreman levels. Everybody knew more because I encouraged them to learn what was going on.

The effect on the customers was that they got their shipment early or when they wanted it. There were fewer quality problems. Quality was built into the product by having the parts available. The worker was able to perform his work in an orderly manner, not in a hurry on overtime. As a result, our reputation was enhanced, and it helped us against our competitors, which made our sales people happy.

In short, I created a three-year program to teach the supervisors at every level of the manufacturing organization how to properly and consistently lead their functional area. We established expectations, and when they were met, we set new ones.

For years, the managers at every level were satisfied with the status quo, and it cost the company dearly, but no one had realized it. Until we analyzed the pattern of inefficiencies using all the information within the organization, there were no expectations to balance production and realize the benefits of a rational program. In other words, prior to the implementation of the Balanced Production Program, the managers had never taken ownership of their parts of the business. This is the job of every successful leader—to get every employee to take ownership of his or her responsibilities.

In the end, GE realized significant operating benefits to balancing its production schedules, including

- a 10–12 percent increase in manufacturing productivity;
- less overtime and idle time due to fewer parts shortages and fewer quality problems; and
- lower shipping costs.

There were also significant improvements outside manufacturing, less overtime in other functions, improved profitability and cash flow, improved customer satisfaction, and improved inter-functional communication.

Learning More about Costs, Pricing, and Market Value

In addition to learning about the effect of balanced production on cash flow, I learned another valuable lesson about market economics during my time in Erie.

My boss often involved me in interactions with customers, and I learned a lot from him. During one particularly unforgettable experience, we had built and shipped two major identical pieces of electrical equipment to an important customer. As it was being installed, a fire occurred at the customer's plant, and our pieces of equipment were damaged. The damaged equipment was shipped back to our factory, and we estimated the price for making the repairs and renewing the warranty. After we drew up the estimate, the customer sent their purchasing agent to discuss the terms.

The customer's purchasing agent arrived for the meeting. After introductions and small talk, we got down to the business at hand. The purchasing agent asked, "What is the price for repairing the damage and renewing the warranty?"

My boss told him the estimate with the price we had worked up for the new contract. He looked up at my boss.

My boss paused briefly, looking back, and without missing a beat, he said, "Each."

I remained still and watched the transaction, knowing how the estimate had been calculated. The purchasing agent agreed to the terms, thanked us, and departed.

After he left, I asked my boss, "Why did you double the price by saying 'each'?"

"He never blinked," he responded.

What a lesson! Pay attention to the details in any negotiation. Look at body language, check your instincts, probe for expectations, and use any ethical opportunity to maximize profit.

This served me well later in my career as I negotiated with international customers.

As I learned more about the pricing side of the equation with experiences like the warranty negotiation, I also learned more about the cost side when we put a plant in Dothan, Alabama, to assemble motors. We opened the Dothan plant to take advantage of the lower costs and better work ethic of the Alabama workforce. In Alabama, we had access to a nonunion workforce, which meant we could pay a lower hourly rate for the factory and office workers. I found that with the flexibility of a nonunion work force, I was able to empower the factory workers and incent them in ways that were not possible when they were "protected" by a union.

In Erie and in many GE locations, the union practice was to pay inspectors a higher rate than the workers assembling the motors. I thought that seemed backward. In Dothan, we explained to the assembly workers that they knew best how to assemble the motors, and it was our expectation that they would assemble them perfectly. The inspectors would only spot-check their work. Therefore, we paid the inspectors a lower rate than the assemblers. The higher pay rate for assembly sent a message to the workers that they were capable and were expected to get it right the first time. This pay-scale adjustment was an early experiment in empowerment, and it worked great.

The Dothan assemblers were a competent lot and did their jobs well. Their pay scale reinforced that the company valued their skills. They lived up to the expectation by turning out a quality product the first time.

Recognition, Promotion, and Moving On

After the Balanced Production Program achieved its goals, my boss was promoted to president of the Canadian subsidiary, and I was given the opportunity to execute the turnaround of another job shop business within GE.

My work in Erie qualified me for something else. When I had arrived in Erie, it was a case of GE hiring me into a position to maintain the status quo. I could have stayed there, gotten all of my raises, and not made any changes because the business was already making good money. There wasn't a perceived problem. I wasn't sent to Erie to solve a problem; I was sent there to fill an open position.

However, I found there was a lot more capability in the Erie business than they were getting out of it by balancing the production line. At that point, I think they said, "This guy Gates might really know what he is talking about."

So they sent me to another plant, this time to Schenectady, New York, with the expectation that I was going to fix the business.

When I went to Schenectady, it was because I had fixed one business from a functional point of view, and so they said, "Okay, hotshot, now do it for the whole business."

My credibility got tested in Erie, and fortunately it worked out. My challenges were about to get bigger.

Chapter 3: Takeaways

1. Reject the status quo.
2. Success is hard work.
3. Any organization can be improved, even good ones.
4. Build a knowledge-based organization.
5. Build accountability into your culture.
6. Think and act like the CEO of your responsibilities.

Chapter 4

Unions, Labor, and Profitability at General Electric in Schenectady

A leadership style must embrace integrity, decisiveness, and open, honest, two-way communication.

Finally, as my last GE assignment, I was promoted to general manager of the large motor and generator department in Schenectady, New York. This time, I was hired into my new position with the expectation that I was responsible for results and was expected to improve them. There was a saying at GE that you haven't worked at GE until you've been through Schenectady. In Schenectady, I got my ticket punched.

Jack Welch, GE's legendary CEO, sat at the top of the corporate pyramid by the time I got to Schenectady. Until Jack, there never was a stated responsibility to improve the performance of each employee in your organization. He insisted on identifying the bottom 5 percent of employees and instituting a plan to improve their performance or move them to another job—or out of the organization. Any readers who were around at that time know the controversy that approach to accountability produced in leadership circles. Jack Welch had the expectation that every leader in his organization had the responsibility to improve the performance of his employees. He set expectations across all lines of responsibility.

In at least the late twentieth century and continuing today, American industry has failed in this regard. US businesses have not been specific in defining expectations for leaders or clear in defining their responsibilities. I believe that this lack of defining specific expectations is one of the main reasons that a status-quo culture leads to stagnation in an organization and allows unproductive practices to embed themselves.

When a CEO sets expectations of all the leaders reporting to him or her, it shakes the culture alive. It requires measurements of success. More importantly, it makes every manager learn the critical success factors in his or her organization. A leader is forced to ask, "What works and what doesn't?" Jack Welch rejected the status quo. He knew instinctively that every business could do better. He expected the leaders of each business to make that happen, and he expected the leaders to improve the performance of all the people in their organizations. I was one of those leaders.

Again, I found poor leadership at the source of a myriad of problems in Schenectady. The previous general manager had simply failed.

One big difference from my previous experience in Erie was this business was losing money when I got there. This situation screamed for a fix; the status quo was unsustainable.

As I mentioned earlier, unlike Erie, my promotion to general manager of the large motor and generator department in Schenectady came with the *expectation* that I would improve the business.

I quickly discovered a number of problems.

The person I replaced had simply "occupied the chair" and enjoyed the perks of office, but he was not involved in managing the business.

I found, though, that his direct reports were competent and willing, so I was welcomed by them and their employees. However, the factory workers were a different story. I learned very early into my tenure there that they were going to present a challenge. While they were in a different union than the workers in Erie – by this time, the International Electrical Workers' Union had supplanted the UEW—they were aware of my reputation in Erie, so they were not particularly happy with my appointment.

The LM&G Department was spread out in five factory buildings. Employees were required to wear hard hats when on site. On my first tour of the factories, I was introduced to the hostile environment in which I would be operating. As I walked around to survey the plant and be introduced to the employees, workers turned their backs to me. The overhead-crane operators dropped steel nuts and bolts on my hard hat, betting who would make the first direct hit. I found out later that they held a lottery for the operator who made the most direct hits. Obviously, the UEW in Erie had communicated their strike experience with me to their fellow union workers in Schenectady. Their actions put me on notice about what I faced in my new role.

My reputation of "that crazy bastard" obviously preceded me. Fortunately, my Erie experience was good training for dealing with angry union workers, so I was unaffected by this treatment and ready for what was to come later.

In Schenectady, I dealt with the IUE. They were tough, but at least they were patriotic. And it was my belief that you had to be tough back.

In addition to the hostility of organized labor, I rather quickly identified several problems in the LM&G business:

1. The hydro generator product line, a significant part of the business, was bleeding money.
2. The productivity of the factory employees was unsatisfactory.
3. Our customer service had deteriorated, and some of our customers were angry.
4. GE had a centralized sales force, and each year, our business negotiated the number of FTE's

(full-time equivalents) we wanted. Related to our poor customer service, their enthusiasm for our business had deteriorated.

5. There were functional silos with too little horizontal communication.

With this range of problems—financial, productivity, cultural, marketing, and sales—I needed to make immediate and substantive changes.

Exiting an Unprofitable Product Line

My first focus was on the hydro generator product line. I was fortunate that I had a very competent and straight-talking finance manager. He did a thorough financial analysis and compared our costs with our Japanese competitor's pricing methodology. Our competitor was able to bid their price at our variable cost. With our high fixed costs, we had no way to compete with them. So I went "up the line" and got approval from our corporate officers to exit the product line. That decision, while difficult, was not the toughest part of the job, but it set the tone that things had changed.

By exiting a product line, it led to massive layoffs, which caused disruption in the shops and more friction with the union. This disruption lasted a rather long time as, per our union contract, a worker's length of service was the factor in "bumping" workers with less service across all GE organizations in Schenectady. By exiting the large hydro generator line, I had to lay off six hundred of the two thousand employees in our factory—yes, about a third of the workforce.

During this time, the union workers would walk out of (strike) one of our buildings one day per week. In practice, this meant that the workers would actually stay home or go to the union hall. While these walkouts were disruptive to our business, we were still able to meet our responsibilities to our customers, which spoke to the low productivity and extra costs in the business I inherited. We had too many people if these walkouts ceased.

Then the unexpected happened. I received a death threat; the union workers threatened to shoot me. My boss ordered me to stay out of the plant until he gave me the "all clear." After a few days, I decided that the union was winning, and that was unacceptable to me. So three days after being told to stay home, I went back in to work. My boss, who was in Nashville, found out that I went back to the plant against his wishes.

By appearing to cower at home, I thought we were playing right into the unions' hands. But, as my boss, that was not his first concern; it was the safety of me and my family.

He called me at the office and said, "Gates, you're close to getting fired. Get the hell out of there until I tell you to go back."

I went home but felt he was wrong.

He caved in and did exactly what the union wanted him to do. I believe to this day that if I had stayed at the office, they would not have shot me, and we would have won sooner. The union threats against my life lasted no more than a week. When the threats ended, I went back in, and as far as I was concerned, we went back to business as usual.

At about the third year of my stay and sometime after the union layoffs, when improvements in our business were noticeable, a senior union official came into my office and shut the door. He was a good guy, and I liked him.

"Have a chair," I said and offered him coffee. He acccpted. "What can I do for you?" I asked.

After exchanging pleasantries, he said, "Mr. Gates, we really believe that you are trying to fix this business, so we're going to support you, but you are *selected*, and we are *elected*, so it won't be without some bumps in the road. It's not going to be all honey and roses. But I am going to help you."

"Thank you." I smiled at the admission. "I look forward to working with you. Let's stay in touch."

We stood and shook hands.

We did stay in touch, and he did help me. We fixed that business. He knew, in the end, that people were going to have jobs because I put the business back on a profitable footing. He agreed that we couldn't keep those six hundred people in a business that was losing money. As a result of laying off six hundred people, we saved the rest of the jobs, and ultimately the union recognized it. The union shop steward knew that there comes a time when you have to let common sense overtake misplaced pride, so common sense prevailed.

> *Think of the many, not of the one.*

Until the union official's visit, the union workers continued to strike one of our buildings each week, every week, staying out for one day. After his visit, things improved at a slightly faster pace. The walkouts phased out and finally stopped, cooperation between the foremen and workers improved, and life was good. I was able to spend more time with customers, fine-tuning the operation, and turning my attention to making the enterprise profitable again.

I had learned early in my career that you have to earn respect. If you get respect, love will come later. A lot of people want to be loved first, and they don't get respect. But I earned respect by doing the right thing. Some people hated me, but they still respected me. And as you get to the transition point between respect and love, you will get people who believe in you. Of course, there will always be a few who don't believe in you, and you have to be ready to deal with that too.

> *If you get respect, love will come later.*

　　　　Elmer D. Gates

I never reported directly to Jack Welch, who, by then, was CEO, but he was a strong leader and set the tone at the company. He had a guiding principle about business that was the undergirding for the kinds of tough decisions I faced in exiting the hydro generator market: "Always run your business with a great deal of emotion and no sentiment."

Before I arrived in Schenectady, the prior leadership made decisions with some sentiment, hence there had been hesitancy regarding exiting this iconic GE hydro turbine generator product line. However, since it was clear we were losing money, as far as I was concerned, necessity made the decision obvious. I was not going to head up a losing product line.

Other divisions went the way of the dinosaur too during that time. We had been in Pittsfield, Massachusetts, for a long time making transformers, and we had been in places like North Carolina—in towns all over the country where we were part of the fabric of the local economy— in businesses that had begun to lose money, or their products could be built at lower cost elsewhere.

Some people said, "Oh, no, we can't leave those communities."

But Jack said, "Yes, we can."

Ultimately, Jack's great emotional commitment to GE's viability trumped sentiment and led to the success the company experienced under his leadership.

Reviewing the Remaining Business

After exiting the unprofitable hydro generator line, I attacked our manufacturing productivity. I had learned lessons doing the Balanced Production Program in Erie that were helpful during this next assignment.

After a couple of meetings with the manufacturing leadership, I realized that—just as I had found in Erie— the various levels of leadership lacked knowledge of their operation. In the "bumping" that occurred after the layoff, the process required that seniority determines which employees are displaced. Bumping meant a lot of employees moved into new jobs, which had a negative impact on productivity. I hired an outside firm on a performance-based contract to improve the productivity of our various shops. While I would not usually hire consultants, moving this responsibility to outsiders allowed me to focus on other major issues within the business. It proved to be a good decision. The results-based contract drove immediate progress. I held weekly reviews with the consultant, and in a short time, we saw an improvement in productivity. We continued the contract for some time until the results were solidified and the manufacturing operation was a more knowledgeable and flexible unit.

During my initial assessment I found the engineering and marketing organizations were quite competent but such was not the case in sales. We had, on too many occasions, let our field sales force down by missing deliveries, shipping defective products, and otherwise disappointing our customers. So I turned my attention to improving customer relations, which required substantive changes in their experiences with our company.

First, I focused on rebuilding relations with the field sales organization. GE had a corporate-level, extremely competent field sales organization, and every year, each department had to negotiate the number of FTE's (full-time equivalents) from the unified sales force. The number of equivalents was only part of the equation; equally important was the enthusiasm for and loyalty to your business of the individual salesmen. If your business was doing a bad job, they weren't particularly anxious to sell your product. As a result, you had a hard time motivating FTEs if you had poor delivery schedules and quality problems.

Our business had disappointed the individual salesmen, which required us to rebuild our credibility with them. Fortunately, there was a scheduled meeting of the entire sales organization shortly after I arrived. I met with them, outlined my approach to fixing the business, and invited them to call me with any problems or opportunities they encountered.

Then my marketing manager and I met with our responsible district sales manager to understand exactly where we were letting the customers down. Next, we promised the DSM that those days were behind us, and he could trust that we would make and meet our commitments on delivery and quality. The DSM accepted my word and asked me to address the entire sales force at a meeting in the near future. I accepted his invitation.

So, at the invitation of the DSM, I gave the sales force a presentation at their meeting, similar to the one I had given him individually. During the breaks, reception, and dinner, I got to know the salesmen who sold our products. I personally gave each one my card and told them, "Call me whenever you have a problem or get a customer request you want to discuss."

This head-on networking approach impressed them, and they quickly figured out there was "a new sheriff in town." I used the opportunity to show them we could deliver by showing up and giving my word that things were going to improve. It was a risk I had to take, and now I had to make sure we delivered on our promise.

At that same meeting, I also asked salesmen to set up meetings with our major customers and to include themselves, myself, and my marketing manager. I put travel on my agenda to support customer sales. This was a major departure from the activity of the previous armchair GM, so that sent another good message that change was here—and it was for the better.

As mentioned earlier, we negotiated for our sales force every year. We would ask for a certain number— say, "I want eleven FTEs" —of people to represent and promote our product line in the marketplace. When the sales force began to see the positive improvements and changes in our department, it was a lot easier for me to get an unfair share of time from the individualized salesmen in the centralized sales force. Obviously, this created a cycle of positive growth as our improved product and customer relations increased the enthusiasm of the people selling it.

I soon had an opportunity to respond to a problem facing the sales force. As I found earlier, the engineering organization was quite good. It had very good technical leadership, and as we executed our new approach, the engineering manager also became a good leader.

Change was underway within our business in Schenectady, but the old leadership structure remained in place elsewhere. This was obvious during one particular situation when one of our large motors failed for a significant customer, a paper manufacturer.

The customer called a company officer to state his unhappiness with the motor failure. The officer called and asked me to accompany him to visit the customer. He said he would pick up me and the district sales manager at Schenectady Airport to fly us to the customer's site for a settlement meeting.

Before we left, the district sales manager and I had arrived at what we determined was a fair settlement. We had developed a strategy for achieving this settlement. I told the corporate officer that we had a plan. As events unfolded, it turned out that we didn't need it.

"Never mind that," he said. "I will pick you up in a company plane and you'll join me to visit the customer."

The senior VP didn't want to hear about our strategy.

We met him at the airport, boarded the corporate jet, and enjoyed a nice breakfast, with all the coffee we wanted, served by a neatly uniformed steward during our flight to the customer site. The senior vice president hid behind his *New York Times* and wanted no discussion on our strategy.

Upon arriving at the customer's office, we made introductions and exchanged pleasantries. Then the customer proposed a settlement that both the district sales manager and I thought was totally unfair. Without asking for an opportunity to caucus and discuss the customer's proposal with us, the corporate officer accepted the offer on the spot. It was a number triple the amount the district sales manager and I had discussed. The deal was struck.

We left the customer's office, drove back to the airport, got on the plane, and flew back to Schenectady. On our return flight, we ate a nice lunch, again served by the steward. Meanwhile, my DSM and I were stunned. After we were seated on our flight and the plane took off, I told the corporate officer, "I will never fly on a company plane again."

He looked a little surprised and somewhat puzzled.

"You fly in luxury," I told him. "You have steak for lunch on your corporate jet. It gives you a false sense of reality. You ride in luxury, are transported by a company car, and you spent a hell of a lot of my money that we didn't need to spend and that we don't have. You just settled for a lot more money than we had to. I work too damn hard trying to turn our business around, and you are giving it away!"

As for solving the technical failure of the motor, the conventional wisdom was that the coil that failed was a manufacturing error. The theory was that it was a coil-winding defect. However, I found that theory peculiar. With my manufacturing background and loyalty to my manufacturing department, I said I didn't believe that was the cause of the failure. I was a one-man minority, but fortunately, I was also the boss. I believed that something like a power surge had burned through the insulation. I knew the coil-winding process, and I knew the people who operated the machinery. I could not believe that with just one coil out of twelve being bad, only one would have been wound defectively.

So I hired the GE service shops to recreate the event and get the power input information on the day the failure occurred. It took a few weeks to schedule the service shop personnel and get approval from the customer to get access to historical data on the day of the failure. It was a complex procedure, but it was worth it. During the day and time of the failure, the service shop studied the incoming current to the motor. As it turned out, the test showed that at the day and time of the failure, there was a huge surge in the electrical current servicing the motor.

That surge was powerful enough to burn the insulation between the layers of the coil, and it was the power spike that caused the coil to short out and the motor to fail.

The study proved worth it—not financially because the corporate officer had already agreed to the egregious settlement. However, it showed the factory workers that I believed in them. Also, it told the engineers, who had accepted the story that the factory was at fault, that they needed to be more thorough and make the *right* decision when they encountered a problem, not just accept the easy or first one!

Shortly after this incident, I was approached by an executive recruiter who was looking for a CEO to turn around a failing manufacturing company in Pennsylvania. I knew that I could stay at GE, so I had to make the difficult decision whether to leave GE after a thirty-plus-year satisfying career for the opportunity to fix a company serving the global cement and mining markets. I could remain in place, comfortably sail into retirement, collect my gold watch, and retire to the Adirondacks. Or I could take on a bigger challenge. Quite simply, after a few conversations with the recruiter, I opted for the bigger challenge.

At my going-away party, the manager of engineering presented me with a miniature version of the failed coil mounted on a base with the inscription, "The Gates Phenomenon." It was a meaningful gesture and a treasured award. I knew they appreciated my teaching them about decision-making in a respectful way.

Even more poignant was the contrast between my first factory tour—which occurred shortly after I arrived in Schenectady, when the overhead crane operators dropped nuts and bolts on my hard hat—and my final good-bye walkthrough. After I had announced my resignation, I made a farewell tour of the factories. I faced quite a different reception than on my first tour.

Instead of dodging hardware, the workers stumbled over one another to get to the main aisle to shake my hand. I got their unspoken message: "Thanks for all you did!"

As if that were not enough to know I was ready for my next, more difficult, and all-encompassing assignment, while packing up my office, my desk phone rang. I picked it up. It was my secretary. "Mr. Gates, Jack Welch is on the line for you."

At first, I chuckled. Those pranksters! My buddies were pulling a fast one on me.

I picked up the receiver.

"Elmer, this is Jack Welch." I recognized his voice. "I want to thank you. You did a hell of job for us. I just want to congratulate you on your new job. And if it doesn't work out and you ever need anything, feel free to call me anytime."

I paused. "Thank you, Jack."[2]

---

[2] That phone call led to my having a lifelong respect for Jack Welch. And it also led to GE getting a lot of motor business after I joined my new company, Fuller Company. I became a great salesman for GE. I had confidence in the quality and value of their motors because I had seen them from the inside. I built them!

Chapter 4: Takeaways

1. Demonstrate quickly that things have changed.
2. Study, learn, and know the total job.
3. Earn respect. Popularity will follow.
4. Run your business with a great deal of emotion but no sentiment.
5. Think of the many, not the one.
6. Lead by example.
7. Make the right decision, not the easy one.
8. Reject the status quo. Defy convention.
9. Success is hard work.

Elmer D. Gates

Part 2

The Three Stages of Organizational Turnaround

Part 2: The Three Stages of an Organizational Turnaround

Leadership Styles for the Stages of a Turnaround

Integrity is important to success in every aspect of life, but it is absolutely critical in a turnaround. In the language of today, "You must walk the walk as well as talk the talk."

You must always say what you mean and mean what you say. Every person in the organization will be judging your performance every day, and their conclusion must be that you are serious, your intentions are honorable and productive, and your decisions support your words.

Decisiveness and taking risks are also important attributes necessary to leading a successful turnaround.

You will need and use all these personal attributes all the time. Meanwhile, the actions that you take will change over time as your organization pulls out of failure and moves toward growth and success. In part 2, I am going to describe how my style changed as the organization responded to the actions I implemented in the turnaround. Some people are more comfortable executing some styles more than others, but a turnaround executive needs all of them in his or her palette of behaviors to be able to move a stagnant organization toward vibrancy.

In the early phase of a turnaround, you will have to make decisions based on the best information available. That information may not be totally accurate, so you need to take associated risks, knowing that if a particular decision turns out to be wrong, you can make another decision to fix it. Make errors of commission, not omission. Failing to make a decision is really making a decision to do nothing. In a turnaround, doing nothing and hoping things get better is the path to failure. Hope is not a strategy!

Communication is necessary and important to individuals, your direct reports, and to groups of stakeholders so you can define expectations, report progress, and deliver both good and bad news. In a turnaround, there are apprehension, rumors, and misinformation. The best way to handle all the uncertainty is to establish regular communication early and maintain it often. It will quell a lot of gossip.

When you first arrive on the scene, be available and visible on all shifts, particularly at the headquarters location. There will be time for communication and visitation with other locations, but your visits to them can wait until after you have started to make the first level of improvement at the main site.

Finally, a positive, can-do attitude is important to developing a culture of success and excellence. In the early days, you will have doubters and even be subject to ridicule, but you need to keep in mind that those attitudes led to the condition you were hired to fix.

The turnaround leader needs to be a cheerleader, find actions individuals took based on your culture change that have made a difference, and celebrate them. This helps instill the new culture of enthusiasm, even while holding people accountable. Eventually, you will create a culture where people want to come to work.

Three Leadership Styles

Beyond the benefits of a successfully turned-around business to shareholders, employees, customers, suppliers, and the community, the person who leads the turnaround reaps many professional development benefits and a sense of pride. The challenges are great, but so are the rewards.

The turnaround leader has the opportunity to guide a business back on the road to success. To successfully navigate the changing environment, the leader employs three distinct leadership styles throughout the duration of the turnaround: the autocratic, or fix-it style; the transition style, which is to delegate and instill the culture of accountability; and finally, the grow-and-prosper leadership style, which is promoting and implementing the ownership and empowerment culture.

You must start with the autocratic, top-down leadership style in the initial phase. During this phase, you establish a temporary culture that tells employees that things have changed; it is no longer business as usual. This is not the time to build relationships, but rather, it is the time to assess and understand the situation and start to change attitudes.

This was an easy style for me to execute. I started to dismantle the culture of comfort that I found. I was able to make low-hanging-fruit improvements quickly while I identified other problems that needed to be fixed. In this phase, I gained about an equal number of believers and doubters. It doesn't matter, though, how many of either group that you get. In the first phase of a turnaround, you need to make decisions and do the right thing without worrying about making friends.

Remember, respect comes first. Love will come later.

As people realize that some things have changed permanently, the next leadership style you use in a turnaround is the transition leadership style. This transition starts when you see small improvements being made and sustained by certain direct reports and others who have demonstrated competence, and you notice some level of commitment to the changes and improvements you are making.

At this stage, it is time to start moving away from centralized command, control, top-down operations, and begin to delegate authority and responsibility. In this phase, you will begin building a culture of accountability in the organization. You must clearly communicate the results you expect and the dates of interim milestones. Make clear that there are consequences for failure. For this to be successful, you also need to gain acceptance of the task and schedule by the individual getting the assignment. Open, honest, two-way communication is required.

Follow-up with your direct reports is critical in the transition phase of a turnaround in order to reinforce the accountability culture.

The transition phase was the most difficult for me. I liked being a dictator. During this phase, you begin to delegate. You must make difficult decisions, and by this time many employees are scared or downright hostile. Any new initiative is greeted with suspicion and hostility. Things are uncomfortable for many employees. Many think that every change will lead to more layoffs.

Everything has a cost, and the decisions and actions you are required to take during the transition phase are the cost of fixing the business. I was never able to repair some of the broken relationships from this phase, but I did successfully lead through the transition to the next, much more enjoyable leadership challenge.

The next and final phase is the most fun and rewarding. It is the grow-and-prosper phase, during which you reposition the company as a viable and leading competitor in the marketplace. Having initiated a culture of accountability, this next step asks employees to take ownership of their responsibilities and empowers them with decision-making authority. It requires an empowerment leadership style because you are creating a company with employees who have ownership mind-sets about their parts of the business.

The grow-and-prosper phase requires the leader to invest time in communicating and training employees to acquire the skills they need to make the right decisions they have been given the authority to make. They must learn to plan their work and work their plans. You also will communicate frequently in this phase, reminding employees about the authority they have been given. Very importantly, at this point, you must spend time listening to what your employees are telling you to determine if they have the skills to make those decisions.

When you have come this far, you now have to build and maintain a culture of ownership and empowerment. It is hard work. Building and maintaining the culture is the responsibility of the CEO, and it is one of the most important and difficult responsibilities of the job. It cannot be delegated.

As you enter the grow-and-prosper phase, your vision becomes longer range. You can focus more on planning and less on doing because you now have others in the organization who understand your expectations of them. By now, most of them are focusing on meeting those expectations and fulfilling their responsibilities, leaving you to do more thinking about how to drive the business forward. They, too, are spending more time planning and less time doing.

Successful businesses need leaders at all levels to do planning. As we reflected back on the materials shortages before the balanced production in Erie, we found that leaders needed to empower employees to plan their work. Those empowered employees must, in turn, demonstrate to their leaders that they employ long-range thinking and planning about their own parts of the business.

In this next section, I will lead you through the way I applied all the phases of U-turn Leadership principles as I took a failing global business and turned it into a world-class competitor.

Chart: Three Stages of U-Turn Leadership styles

TURNAROUND STAGE	LEADERSHIP STYLE
1. **FIX-IT STAGE (REPAIR)**	Autocratic Leadership • Top-down • Centralized control • Decisive
2. **TRANSITION STAGE (PREVENTION)**	Delegation and Leadership Development • Accountability • Inclusion • Employee ownership: CEO of your area of responsibility • Employees own their performance
3. **GROW-AND-PROSPER STAGE (MAINTENANCE)**	Empowerment and Creativity Leadership • Constantly set new expectations • Decisions close to the action • Entrepreneurial mind-set of the employees • Employees may strike out to establish businesses or divisions • Knowledge and learning organization

Elmer D. Gates

Chapter 5

U-Turn Assignment: What You'll Find

Instead of watching things happen, you want to get in front and make things happen.

The experiences and lessons I gained starting with reengineering the pontoon bridge in Korea to increasing productivity on a manufacturing line to exiting an unprofitable product line could be applied to any business, including this next global business. By instilling a culture of rejecting the status quo at my next assignment, our group was able to not only fix the company, but we transformed a global company into a world-class company as well—two decidedly different things.

Turnarounds require bold, decisive, and quick action. Before you take action, though, you need to move into your new position and take a quick but thorough look around.

The Job They Hired Me to Do

The executive recruiter who wooed me from General Electric made a compelling argument that convinced me to take on the challenge to turn around a global manufacturer serving the cement and mining industries—Fuller Company in Bethlehem, Pennsylvania. Fuller was owned by GATX, a conglomerate headquartered in Chicago. The recruiter pointed out that even if I failed, which he figured was quite a possibility given the dire situation I found, I would be in the marketplace looking for a job at a whole new level—the CEO level—at a whole new salary level, too.

I was ready for the move and decided to take the calculated risk.

⋮

I was not the only person from GE who had interviewed for the position of CEO at Fuller Company. GATX had also interviewed a GE marketing executive but because of the board's misunderstanding of the problems within their organization, they hired me based on my manufacturing experience to address the kinds of problems they *thought* they had.

One cautionary note before you start your turnaround assignment: the people hiring you may have no idea of the real problems facing the company or, worse yet, have a false reading of the problem.

Fuller Company was primarily in the cement-plant business. We designed them, we built them, we shipped them to sites around the globe, and we assembled them when they arrived at their destination. Then we provided ongoing support for maintenance. When I arrived at Fuller, the company held a paltry 3 percent of its global served market, which during the 1980s, excluded certain countries with whom we did not transact business, such as the old Soviet Union, Iran, and Cuba. But for the most part, we had a global footprint that took us to all parts of the world.

How Did Fuller Fall So Low?

A business rarely ever goes from healthy to unhealthy in a short period of time. Most often, there is a string of small and seemingly insignificant negative actions or inactions that, in the judgment of management, do not require remedial action. A series of such events over time will ultimately create the need for a turnaround. Businesses in this situation can be at any stage of development from early stage to mature companies.

In the case of Fuller, the company was founded in 1928 by Colonel James W. Fuller III shortly after he sold the successful Lehigh Car, Wheel, and Axle business that had been started by his father, James W. Fuller Jr. Fuller Company was a natural outgrowth of Fuller's other business interests in cement, steel, and iron, so the founders were well-integrated into its industry, and the company was advantageously located in an area with a strong cement history. The American cement industry was born in Pennsylvania's Lehigh Valley, an area with limestone so pure it was dubbed "cement rock." In 1959, Fuller was acquired by GATX Corporation headquartered in Chicago, Illinois, so it had deep corporate support, but its management remained independent.

I was entering an entrenched firm with a strong history. Fuller had been successful in its early years or it would not have been around when I arrived. But whatever had worked in the past had long since ceased to be successful.

The person I replaced stayed with the business for a few months before moving to corporate headquarters. During this time, I had to respectfully reverse decisions he had made and actions he had taken in my effort to begin to move the company forward. I met with little resistance, which was helpful. He was a gentleman, and his demeanor allowed me to do my job.

Obviously when a company needs a turnaround, it is a failure of leadership, but that is an over simplification. As mentioned at the beginning of this book, it's a failure on at least two levels of leadership—the CEO and the board of directors. This raises the issue of the selection of directors and the need to establish a "statement of expectations" for the positions of directors and chairman of the board. It also argues for regular evaluation of the board as a whole, for individual directors, and for the CEO. In a turnaround situation, and in all business situations, nobody should get a pass.

In examining any failure of leadership, one or several of the following conditions exist:

- lack of focus on external environment
- inept, distracted, or uninvolved leadership
- an internal focus
- a culture of comfort and satisfaction
- lack of creativity
- lack of excitement
- poor execution

All of these problems existed at Fuller to some degree in every corner of the business. The opportunities for change were obvious and many; the question was how many, how fast, and how soon could I make them?

As was my aggressive style, I made them fast, soon, and all across the board.

Preparing for the First Day

My years at GE prepared me to take the reins with authority—quickly and decisively.

I made a mental list of what needed to happen to disrupt the status quo. I told myself

1. You own the business; act like it! Forget everything else. It is your business to fix.
2. Prepare to work 24/7/365. Be prepared to sacrifice personal time, social, and even family events and vacations. You're on duty.

3. Set the tone that "effective right now, things have changed." Then make sure they do!
4. Consider long-range planning as a twenty-four-hour cycle.
5. Have a plan for getting started, then be prepared to change it as you begin to learn the operation and the people.

There is No "Honeymoon Period" in a Turnaround

You need to get started. Like saving a drowning boatload of summer workers, time is not on your side. Any successful turnaround needs to ramp up quickly and be well-established within the first six months of your tenure. Energy and enthusiasm for the task are essential. Indecision is not your friend.

Know Your People

You'll be fighting some entrenched people, processes, and practices:

- a casual attitude toward work and a lack of excitement, enthusiasm, energy and creativity
- a lack of firm commitment to meeting schedules internally and externally; excuses are acceptable.
- rigid functional silos with little horizontal communication; little sharing of information

- lack of crispness in execution, resulting in quality and customer service challenges
- "unofficial" or "coffee-machine" leaders, most having negative views about the company and management. They are very vocal "undercover communicators." They are cancerous to the organization. Cure them or can them.
- similarly, since failing organizations suffer a leadership void at the top and nature abhors a vacuum, others will attempt to fill that leadership void. Identify the person(s) filling this void and evaluate which team they are on.

Stop the Bleeding

While you are getting to know your people, you will also be looking at the hard facts and the numbers. You need to find out exactly *where* the business is bleeding money and *why* it is bleeding money.

I told myself, "You own the business. Act like it." What owner doesn't look at his or her books? First and foremost, can you pay your bills? Are your customers paying their invoices? Are your employees working a full-day's work for a full-day's pay?

Owning the business required an owner's mind-set. An owner wants to know what his or her people are doing, is always surveying their property, and is always thinking about how to make things better for his or her customers.

For me, the owner's mind-set sounded like this:

- Shed any outside responsibilities that might distract you. Your schedule is 24/7/365, visiting all locations and all shifts unannounced. People are good at "faking it." Hit the ground running.
- Find out what's causing the bleeding. Use financial facts, not opinions. This will help set priorities.
- Be consistent in words, actions, and relationships. Lead by example. Show confidence that you will fix it.
- Send the message that things have changed and that business as usual won't be tolerated.
- Be in a constant evaluating mode of everyone and everything you see. Be prepared to change your mind as you learn more. Evaluate performance, not personality.
- Be skeptical. Many will accentuate the positive. Others will tell you what is wrong; it's never their fault or the fault of their particular organization.
- Get to know people at every level of the organization.
- Analyze the organizational structure of the company and question the rationale for the particular structure.
- Be aware of the culture of the organization and identify the cultural deficiencies that you will need to change. You will find, in most cases, the culture of the organization is a "default culture." Events,

not leaders, have molded the culture; therefore, no one internally defines it.

- Start changing the culture immediately, which requires you to think early and often about the culture you intend to instill in the organization. Remember, culture is the leader's responsibility.
- To change the culture, lead by example, be consistent, and hold people accountable.
- Communicate often with a two-way, top-down, bottom-to-top, open, and honest style. Be a patient and eager listener.
- Find the low-hanging fruit and score early successes. Even small ones count. Former New York City mayor Rudy Giuliani scored high marks early in his first term by eliminating the windshield-washing individuals at the Holland Tunnel. It seemed like a small gesture, but for a world-class destination city that makes a lot of its revenue from tourism, it had an immediate and noticeable impact.
- Practice Management By Walking Around (MBWA). Tom Peters popularized the concept, which he says he picked up from visiting Hewlett-Packard's President John Young in 1978 when he was studying companies who did things well.[3] MBWA will, in a vast majority of turnaround situations, demonstrate a definite shift in management's

---

[3] From Tom Peters' blog, accessed January 13, 2015 at http://tompeters.com/blogs/toms_videos/docs/Excellence_MBWA.pdf

attitude and approach to leading. My experience is that most managers presiding over a failing enterprise tend to be office-bound.

- Recognize that you will have already built fear into a number of employees, ranging from fear of loss of their job to fear of you. Repairing these relationships is a job for the next phase. Remember, with a number of people, fear is a great motivator.

- This discovery phase should last no more than three months. During this period, if you have followed through on the items listed, you will have every employee's attention, and some things are beginning to go correctly already.

Identifying the Real Problem

The people hiring me had concluded that their problem was poor productivity and poor quality. They concluded their abysmal failure was an internal operations problem. I was hired over others because during my time at GE, I had built a reputation for controlling costs, building quality products, improving productivity, and controlling inventory. In short, I was a successful manufacturing executive. Had the executives at Fuller Company and GATX known the real problem, I never would have been hired.

As I started my assignment at Fuller, it became obvious that the real problem was that Fuller had deserted its customers. Management had no knowledge of the status of major projects, particularly those in Egypt, India, Pakistan, and New Zealand. People were not being held accountable for performance. Employees in charge of large, international contracts were remote, hands off, disinterested, and office-bound.

After spending a few decades at GE getting to know and support customers in the field, Fuller employees' laissez-faire attitudes toward their customers were immediately obvious, revealing, and disappointing.

After a month of observing the status quo, I flew to corporate headquarters and told the corporate officers of GATX, "If you have inventory, quality, or productivity problems, I'll fix them. But the real problem is you have lost contact with the customer, and I'm going to fix that first. I'll be doing a lot of international travel, and I'll be fixing problems here at the same time."

Before I began my travels, I collected status reports on the state of the business I had just agreed to fix. I conducted both revenue reviews and project reviews with the responsible vice presidents. What I found was head-shakingly disheartening. The leaders most directly responsible for the performance of certain units and large projects were unaware of some of the essential information they needed to properly and successfully execute their responsibilities. This is the same situation I found at my two GE turnaround experiences. The corporate officers at Fuller did not understand what was really happening, and a couple of them didn't seem to care.

At Fuller, I found four things in common with all other failing organizations:

1. a culture of comfort
2. little discipline
3. poor execution throughout the company
4. customer is an interruption, not an opportunity

Because I had seen this before, from the outset, it was clear that the existing culture needed to be destroyed. I knew it was important to get it done quickly, and it was not important *how* I got it done. I just needed to disrupt the status quo *now*.

My confidence was high. The basics I had learned throughout my career were applicable across all functions here. That's why I was able to move so quickly at Fuller.

Chapter 5: Takeaways

1. Form your own conclusion about the state of the organization. Be wary of the opinions of others and be cautious of any advice you receive.
2. Make things happen. Have a plan for getting started and be prepared to adapt as the situation unfolds.
3. You own the business; act like it! Forget everything else. It is your business to fix. Be decisive!
4. Think and act 24/7/365. Be prepared to sacrifice personal time, social, and even family events and vacations. You're on duty.
5. Set the tone that "effective right now, things have changed." Then make sure they do! Every decision you make, every action you take, and everything you say must reinforce the company culture you are building.
6. Consider long-range planning as a twenty-four-hour cycle.
7. Success is hard work.

Chapter 6

Stage One: The Fix-It Phase

Now that you've surveyed the landscape, met the people, and started to familiarize yourself with the situation, you've entered the fix-it phase. It's time to make big, symbolic changes. These changes will shake up the status quo and set the stage for deeper, more meaningful changes throughout the organization.

In this chapter, we'll look at the actual first steps I took at Fuller to shake up the culture and move things in a new direction.

Harsh Steps, Rapid Change

Your approach to the first days will depend on your experience, personality, and leadership style. While your style is your own, certain actions are essential to turning around a critical situation. It doesn't matter how you do it, as long as you do it!

No matter *how* you do it, make sure you

1. Establish that you are the boss. Be decisive. Set the example and expectation that decisiveness is required of those around you as well.

2. Get a list of all the reports that come to you. Study them at night *starting with the financial reports.* Numbers tell a story; they don't lie. Question the purpose of each report. It will be hard to get an answer about the purpose of each report, and you won't get consistent answers from members of the leadership team. That tells you something about their knowledge and involvement in the business and possibly the value of the report in your hands.

3. Start making changes immediately even though some will involve risk. The faster the change, the faster the improvement starts.

4. Speed is important, and consistency is critical. You are being judged every minute by every employee in the organization. Your words and actions will send signals, and at this point, all eyes are on you. Make sure your words and actions are sending the message you want to send. You want to earn respect. Focus on earning respect and not on being loved. Remember, love will come later!

5. You have to start building a culture of decisiveness and accountability immediately. Set dates and times for meetings and expect everyone to be there with the answers you requested. If your

expectations are not met, coach and correct on the spot. Communicate clearly that answers are expected on the time and date requested and that there are consequences for nonperformance. This sends a message that change is underway and accountability is in vogue.

Even though you are there to fix a business and not win a popularity prize, you also know that you are operating in a political environment. You have power, and you have to wield it skillfully. To make the transition, I knew I needed enough people so that I could win the political battles. That meant getting to know people and letting them get to know me.

During the Fix-It Phase, they will call you a rotten bastard. Don't worry. You'll get used to it. I would call people into my office for reviews of projects and budgets, and if they didn't give me the right answer, I would fire them on the spot.

At that point, people understand that things are changing. You will get about a quarter of the people on your side. They will be the right 25 percent, and they are all you need to start to turn it around.

The First Power Move

During the first few days, I met with the vice president leadership team and with each vice president individually to gain first impressions. I visited our shops nearby in Allentown, Catasauqua, and Manheim. I walked around the headquarter office to meet the next layer of management and the employees (draftsmen, purchasing agents, lawyers, etc).

Office hours started at 8:00 a.m., and I arrived at the office at around 7:30 a.m. At first, I had no company. After about a month, a couple of vice presidents showed up and came into my office to chat. We talked mostly about business. These were the ones that "bought in" to what I was doing first. Then I started coming to work at 7:00 a.m., and again some people followed suit. I didn't do it to intentionally move up everyone's start time. I came to work early to plan the day. However, people started to follow my lead. Clearly, I had started to set the tone that I was leading by example.

As far as the rest of the employees, in the first couple of weeks, I saw that employees were too casual about starting work on time. Starting time for everyone was 8:00 a.m., and many would arrive between 8:15–8:45 a.m. For many, their first action upon arrival was to get a cup of coffee in the cafeteria.

This was unacceptable. Their casual attitude unfortunately carried over to their attitude toward their responsibilities. It also was a clue that we might be overstaffed.

So one day, I told the maintenance supervisor, "Lock all the doors at a couple of minutes before 8:00 a.m."

"Huh?" he looked at me quizzically, but he locked the doors.

My purpose? Let people know that things have changed!

This action set expectations in a direct and forceful way. In fact, if it hadn't been so serious, it would have been funny to hear all the phones ringing around the building, with locked-out employees calling from pay phones and asking what was going on. Remember, this happened a decade before people carried personal cell phones. Many who picked up our phones internally had the answer. Others guessed.

"It's that crazy guy in the corner office."

At 8:30 a.m., I opened the doors and sent a memo to all employees, reinforcing the fact that we were a global company with global customers and suppliers and that our job was to serve our customers. We couldn't do that if we weren't at work. That action had an immediate and positive effect. People arrived in time to be ready to work at 8:00 a.m. People still speak about that episode thirty years later, so it was memorable as well as effective.

To: All Employees

From: Elmer Gates

The reason the doors were locked this morning is because we need to be here on time to be ready to respond to any calls from customers, potential customers, suppliers, or anyone in the community. Please be at your desk at 8:00 a.m., ready to serve our customers.

Thank you for your cooperation.

In my previous turnaround successes, I learned that you can't force people to want to come to work. The reason many of them were late was that they were getting no real job satisfaction. Work was drudgery. To build a workforce eager to get to work, people need to feel gratification and recognition. The company culture has to be fun, or at least exciting, while meeting or exceeding customer's expectations every day. We needed to show our employees that their work was important to the customers, and we did that in the next phase of the turnaround.

It would take time to get there, but we would. Change had begun.

> *Build a culture where people want to come to work.*

Big, Symbolic Change

Things also had to change physically.

Over several years, an elitist attitude had become firmly entrenched in the executive suite. The leadership was out of touch, not only with the customers but with their own employees as well. Employees felt the divide too. They were working for "the man." They weren't working for the customers or themselves. They didn't take ownership of their responsibilities, and they were relegated to a separate caste within the company.

To destroy the culture of comfort, I made a big, symbolic change that sent a message both to the elitist leadership and to the disengaged employees. The executive suite had been set apart from the rest of the office space by large, floor-to-ceiling, wooden doors. Employees never entered these imposing doors, and leaders, quite frankly, hid behind them.

Enough of that. I called the building maintenance supervisor again.

"Remove these doors," I told him.

The building maintenance personnel surveyed the doors and said, "Sorry, sir. We can't remove them. If we take them down, it will interfere with the operation of the air-conditioning system."

"We can fix the damn air conditioning," I said. "Take down the doors."

The doors were removed. The air conditioning worked fine, and employees who had never stepped over the threshold into the executive suite were welcomed there. I sent a memo inviting the employees to come in and visit. At first, there was caution, but in a fairly short time, they became comfortable.

The entrenched, elite leadership got the message that they weren't hiding behind big, wooden doors anymore, and the workers got the message that they mattered. With the caste system shattered and physical barriers removed, it was time for people to get to work to fix the business.

Connecting with the Customer

Taking into consideration that we were a global manufacturer of heavy equipment, I expected to find a global mind-set among the leadership and the project managers who were responsible for the success of the business. That global mind-set was lacking when I arrived. Instead, the local, insular Pennsylvania-Dutch culture was prominent.

Company leaders had become accustomed to a comfortable lifestyle while leading a failing enterprise. Some corporate officers with global-project responsibilities had never visited customer sites, therefore they had no accurate understanding of local working conditions, the attitude of customer executives, and no real measure of our site supervisors' effectiveness; they had no accurate status of their own projects. They reported that everything was on track based on reports from the field, yet we were losing money.

At a staff meeting early in my tenure, I told my direct reports that my observation was that the most significant decisions they made each day were deciding at what temperature their secretaries set the thermostat and which secretary would bring their lunch.

Meanwhile, their travels mostly involved attending industry trade meetings in the United States and taking their wives on business trips and entertaining each other. International travel by executives was largely company-paid vacations for executives and their wives. I stopped that.

I found the same elitist attitude among the presidents of our foreign companies. The foreign executives had a cushy existence, great salaries and benefits, expense accounts with little oversight, and no expectations for improving their operations. On rare occasions when US executives visited them, these executives were well entertained.

On my first trip to Paris to visit our company there, I sent a fax ahead of my arrival to an officer of our French company, outlining what I intended to accomplish during my stay. Nonetheless, when I arrived, after brief introductions, his first words were, "What attractions would you like to see, Elmer?"

"I would like to visit the President of Cement Français," I replied.

After a quick review of our French operation, he and I left in his car to visit the customer. He got lost. We were late for the meeting.

When we returned to the office, I told him, "You obviously haven't spent much time calling on the customer." I terminated him.

Similarly, a president of one of our subsidiaries flew first class on his trips to the United States. His first stop was San Francisco, where he would spend three days recovering from "jet lag." He had an air of undeserved arrogance. I decided to visit him.

His office reflected his persona. He had a bar in his conference room and a company-paid membership to an upscale "businessman's club" in the area.

"Our company policy is that we do not allow alcohol in our facilities," I informed him.

"I invite customers on Fridays to socialize," he responded.

"Use the club, but there is to be no alcohol on the company premises," I repeated.

After I returned to the United States, I monitored the performance of his company. His results were unacceptable. I gave him short-term expectations and explained the consequences of failing to meet them. I added, "From now on, travel business class and no jet lag R&R when you arrive in the United States."

His performance did not improve. I terminated him and replaced him with a real leader.

This elitist behavior was repeated throughout the company at all levels of management.

Like any industry, the cement industry had industry associations. Our sales people and selective VPs attended with the ostensible intent of getting to know our customers better in onc-on-one meetings. At the first such meeting I attended with our sales manager, we hosted two customer executives at an upscale restaurant. At a nearby table, two senior executives were entertaining their wives. No customers were evident at their table. They were spending company money with a negative return. Upon return to the office, I wrote another memo.

To: VPs and Sales Managers
From: Elmer Gates
Re: Industry Association Meetings

Effective immediately, all trade-association-meeting attendance is limited to employees; wives will not be in attendance either at company expense or your own. Further, employees who are not working at our booth or hosting our hospitality suite are expected to be entertaining customers at dinners or shows. Attendance is work, not a perk for wives. We are at meetings to connect with our customers and benefit the company.

I will approve attendance at all future industry association meetings.

E. D. Gates

I made it clear that business trips were simply that. More change!

My First Project-Review Meeting

I held project-review meetings covering each one of our projects. At our first meeting, one project manager had finished his first project review.

"I want to review the next project," I said to him.

He looked uncomfortable. "Let me get my assistant project manager to give you an update," he said.

"If you need your assistant to report the status, bring him in. We don't need you! Go clean out your desk," I responded. He stood frozen. I continued, "If you have an open expense account, we'll send a reimbursement check to you, along with your final paycheck."

Message sent: you have to be accountable.

A lesson from my previous experiences was that the assistants helped their bosses maintain their comfortable lifestyles and avoid being accountable. Salaries for assistants at any level are a cost no business can afford.

I removed the extra layer. Those who were in charge now knew what it meant to be a vice president, project manager, or senior manager within Fuller Company.

My First Revenue Review

If the project review is the key to customer service, the revenue review is both the start and a key to the budget process.

At my first revenue review, I called in the person responsible for spare-parts sales. I knew from my years at GE that spare parts sales are a manufacturing company's profit generator and cash cow. The spare parts division is the most profitable sector of the business, so an accurate revenue projection is critical. This was an important review.

I asked the spare-parts sales manager for his forecast for next year. After all, much of our financial viability depended on his accurate assessment of his part of the business.

"Tell me about your forecast for next year," I said.

"We did X last year and should be able to improve that by four percent next year," he told me confidently.

Fair enough. I was new here. I wanted detail so I could understand the basis for his projections.

"How did you arrive at those numbers?" I asked, genuinely curious about how we determined how the cement industry was performing.

After all, the quantity and timing of spare parts revenue depends mostly on which of the cement manufacturing companies are having a plant shutdown to do major maintenance. To prepare for a maintenance shutdown, customers order a lot of spare parts. It would follow, then, that the man knew which customers were anticipating maintenance shutdowns, when the shutdowns would occur, and what parts were likely to be required to service those customers' facilities to meet their maintenance requirements.

"How much of the increase is volume and how much is price?" I asked. "Are you proposing a price increase? If so, how much?"

He didn't have an answer.

Then I asked, "Which companies are having major shutdowns?"

He didn't know.

"Have you talked with our service department?"

He said, "No."

I said, "Obviously you are not in touch with our customers. Go clean out your desk and leave. We'll send you your check."

It was another hard message sent. For Fuller Company to be successful, we needed to have meaningful plans and budgets based on knowledge of our customers' needs and their plans. Here, and unfortunately in too many other parts of the business, this inattention to detail was prevalent.

My First International Customer Call

I received a call from a customer in the Middle East who complained mightily that we had shipped a vital piece of equipment to him with a major defect. I told him I'd call him back ASAP.

I immediately called the responsible individual into my office.

"What is going on with this customer? Explain this situation," I said to him.

"I don't know. My engineer on the project will know," he said.

"Get your chief engineer and come into my office," I told him.

They came to my office and didn't know the problem.

I told the engineer, "Get ready to go to the site and stay there until the customer calls me and tells me that he is satisfied."

Then I faxed the customer (we didn't have computers then) and asked him to fax a letter back to me indicating that he was inviting the engineer to visit his company. Once we had the customer's authorization, the engineer obtained a visa and was on his way the next day.

My phone rang fifty-two days later. It was the customer who called to say the defect was corrected and that he was pleased with the work the engineer did. The chief engineer came home and, frankly, was a changed man. Some good, some bad. He understood that sacrifice was necessary to satisfy a customer, and he wasn't willing to make that sacrifice again. He found opportunity elsewhere.

This swift action sent another clear message to the organization: the customer comes first; no excuses. Beyond that, word got around that vice presidents would be held accountable, as would every employee.

This action earned us favorable treatment by this customer later. We built another complete plant for them. He also told our story to other cement executives in the region, further multiplying the effect of our response.

Our global reputation's rehabilitation had begun.

My Visits to Global Customers

Rebuilding our reputation required that I get on an airplane, something I had grown accustomed to at GE. I anticipated and, in fact, enjoyed meeting with our customers at their locations. After coming to understand the level of customer disengagement at Fuller, my presence was required at customer locations to establish that change had arrived.

Within the first year, I visited four projects in Israel, Egypt, India, and Pakistan. All were behind schedule.

The person in charge of the Indian project was loathe to travel there, and since excuses had been acceptable under prior management, he didn't. When I met with our customer in India, he was understandably upset.

I called the person in charge of the project back in the States. "Get a visa and get on a plane to this project ASAP, and don't come home until I tell you to."

The person in charge of the project had never traveled to India, nor eaten Indian food. The experience intimidated him. He loved Pennsylvania-Dutch food! He packed a supply of candy and snacks in his luggage, got his visa, and jumped on a flight. He returned thirty days later with a different view of the project status. After that, he became a regular visitor to India but continued to carry his own food supply.

We eventually established our credibility with this customer to the extent that we had his unwavering trust. In this instance, the company experienced several delays that held up construction, including a violation of environmental regulations, a strike by the construction workers, and finally, a one-hundred-year flood.

Due to these delays, I told the chairman, "Your plant has gone out of warranty."

He was unconcerned.

"Mr. Gates, you are my warranty," he replied.

Our actions to correct any deficiencies with this customer gave us credibility. This experience speaks volumes about the importance of relationships. Without integrity, you have nothing. With it, you have a solid footing for business relationships that will serve you well.

Next, I arrived in Pakistan to meet with the person in charge there.

"Why are we behind schedule?" I asked. After all, I had traveled halfway around the globe to get some answers.

He blamed the native workers for his problems and delays, using profanity and disrespectful language to describe them, which prevents me from recreating his part of our dialogue here.

"Pack your bags, get a ticket home, and clean out your desk when you get there," I told him.

I couldn't have a representative of our company being so culturally insensitive. He was the stereotypical "ugly American," with a superior attitude and an arrogance that worked against the reputation we wanted to build in every country in which we did business. We were the foreigners. I told all our people in the field that they were the president of Fuller in that part of the world and that our customers would judge our company on their performance. They needed to think and act like a CEO.

The local workers weren't the cause of the delay. It was a lack of project-management leadership. Unfortunately, up until that time, excuses were acceptable answers at Fuller. Now the ship was turning around.

The third stop on my tour of our troubled global job sites led me to Egypt. The Egypt project was suffering a huge cost overrun based partly on a local labor strike, but also, as it turned out, partly due to the lack of a strong site leadership.[4]

I traced the fact that we were losing money and behind schedule to an ineffective leader managing the project. Immediately upon my return home, I sent the responsible corporate officers there to negotiate a new schedule and make other contract modifications with the customer to position the project as a priority for Fuller.

Both men remained in Egypt for two months until a modified schedule and terms were agreed upon by the customer. Upon their return, one of the men retired. He had proven himself to be an ineffective executive. He didn't want to do what I required to meet the customer's expectations.

For my fourth and final visit on my inaugural tour, I visited the project in Israel, a processing plant in the Negev Desert. When you are in the Negev Desert, you are isolated and lonely. The person in charge had told me the customer was very happy with us. When I arrived, I met with the customer and traveled out to the site.

At the job site, I found that I was a president of an organization managing a failed project and leading a

---

[4] I saw a mirage on my trip across the Sahara Desert—trees, pools of water, and other vegetation. What a sight!

lousy company. I was told back in Bethlehem that the customer was very happy with us. As it turned out, the report I received was wrong. When I spoke with the customer's management team on-site, I found that quite the opposite was true.

The customer had a very clear message for me. They were disappointed, not only in the construction of the plant but also our company's slow reaction to concerns they had raised over several months.

This fix-it phase at Fuller reinforced the lesson I learned at GE: managers at every level of their organization do not have in-depth knowledge of their operations. The result is that there is opportunity for improving every organization and converting it to a knowledge-based learning organization.

As it turned out, the customer's plant was a complex problem. A forthright and honest appraisal resulted in my realization that we had sold a process that wouldn't do the job. The piece of equipment in question was incapable of accomplishing the end result. We had sold him a piece of equipment that was the first of its kind, and after this debacle, it was also the last!

With our acknowledgment of the problem, we negotiated a settlement with the customer that included supplying dependable equipment on an expedited schedule. That was another problem solved and another small but positive step in rebuilding our reputation.

A New Fuller

The global tour further sent a message about the new Fuller: The customer comes first. Excuses are unacceptable. The CEO knows the status of each project better than the vice president and the project manager, and that should be and was an embarrassment to them. After all, no employee wants his leader to have a better handle on his part of the business than he does.

These changes came about with expedited overseas travel, renegotiated contracts, and honest appraisals of our shortcomings. Employees and customers knew that the new CEO meant business. I was clearly improving the business.

After the shake-ups in revenue analysis, personnel, and customer service, we achieved

- much closer management at every level of our projects;
- more customer contact by the vice presidents;
- more two-way communication within the organization. Silos were eroding;
- vice presidents learned that they were expected to have accountability and have up-to-date knowledge of each project in their area of responsibility. No more abdication. Delegation, setting expectations, and accountability were the new way of life;

- vice presidents of global projects erred on the side of traveling too much, and they led by example as I did in my global trips; and
- elitism was eradicated.

Employees at Fuller Company were learning some new ways of doing business.

Lead by example at every level. Hold yourself accountable. Oh, and success is hard work and requires sacrifice.

There were a lot of changes between locking the doors at 8:00 a.m. during my first week and traveling the globe to visit our customers. While I established that the status quo was not acceptable and disruption was the new normal during the fix-it phase, the next phase is the hard work of the actual transition where you are putting new, better habits in place.

In the next chapter, we'll talk about what took place during the transition phase at Fuller.

Elmer D. Gates

Chapter 6: Takeaways

1. Make sure that things have changed.
2. Be decisive. If you make a bad decision, make another one to fix it.
3. Execute projects crisply. Reinforce accountability with direct reports.
4. Cultivate cultural sensitivity, appreciation, and respect for your global customers. You represent our company and our country.
5. Hold people accountable. Never relax.
6. Do whatever it takes. Success is hard work.
7. Continue to reinforce the new culture. It's your major responsibility.

Chapter 7

Stage Two: The Transition Phase

Minimize layers in an organization.

During the transition phase, people are on notice that things have changed. You are beginning to know who is on your side. People are actually sorting themselves out. Your believers step up their game. Some people are your detractors and find opportunities elsewhere, others go underground, and most wait and see.

You have destroyed the old culture. People are feeling uncertain, and for those who are paying attention, it is clear that things are changing for the better. At this point, you need to put new processes in place.

Your job is now to start a journey toward building the new permanent culture in the organization. At this juncture, the change process has started. Employees understand that outstanding customer service is a must, that each employee is accountable to complete his or her assignment on schedule, and that the new culture of "never be satisfied, we can do better" is beginning to be embraced by more employees.

Building a New Company Culture

You will recognize that your employees are beginning to embrace the cultural changes you have initiated in areas like customer service and accountability that you have set in motion by your decisive actions. You know by more smiles on employees' faces. The amount of time it takes to arrive at the point of transition to the new culture will depend on the size of your organization. In a small entrepreneurial company, it can take as little as a few meetings in the first months. In a larger company, as I described in previous chapters, it took me five to six months to destroy the old culture and deliver the message that change was here.

This transition phase is more difficult than the fix-it phase for this reason. As I said earlier, it is easy to destroy an old culture that grew by default. Remember, just a few months ago, the culture was one of comfort, inward focus, and functional isolation. Many employees are still looking to return to the good old days. During the transition, you are pulling against the tug to return to the way things were.

You must remain firm. You must also start delegating so that the culture can spread. At this point, you stop dictating to people and start coaching them instead. You stop micromanaging. This was difficult for me since I had great success during the months I had micromanaged.

As I started to delegate, I encountered difficulty because some employees said, "Be careful. He is setting you up to fail so he can fire you." Of course, nothing was further from the truth. I needed allies, lots of them, to successfully turn around the company. But after disrupting their comfortable lifestyle, several, if not more, employees did not trust me. The distrustful ones were always thinking I had an ulterior motive—mainly to cut costs and have another reduction in the workforce. That made the transition phase more difficult than the fix-it phase.

On the other hand, there were a large number of employees who had positive feelings about the changes afoot. Some understood that some action had been needed (even if they believed maybe not quite so severe) while others actually welcomed the changes saying, "It's about time!"

Some never trusted me throughout my entire time with the company. Fortunately, their numbers were very few. I describe them as "coffee-machine leaders." Every company has them; every boss encounters the. Know who they are because, most often, they are your enemies. However, as Sun Tzu[5] says, "If you know your enemy, you can usually win!"

Another leader with a style different than mine— perhaps less confrontational— could have, undoubtedly, achieved the same result, but it may not have been done in the short period it took me.

---

[5] Sun Tzu is a fifth-century BC Chinese warrior whose book, *The Art of War*, is a classic on military strategy. This is only slightly paraphrased. Sun Tzu believed that if you knew your enemy, he or she could be defeated.

With the disruption behind, it was time to start the transition to the new culture.

Christmas in Bethlehem

When my first Christmas in Bethlehem arrived, I anticipated the company Christmas party. In the 1980s, most holiday office parties were called "Christmas parties." It was all the more appropriate now that I was living and working in "The Christmas City."

During my first year, the Fuller Company Christmas party was held in a church-hall basement for some office people. No shop people were invited. I walked down to the basement, decorated with a small tree, some tinsel garland strung around the room, and poinsettias adorning tables topped with paper tablecloths. Workers sat on folding chairs at long banquet tables set up end-to-end. A meal was served family style. And dessert? The church-hall volunteers placed blocks of Neapolitan ice cream on paper plates in front of us.

I stood and gave the company's Christmas welcome and invited the employees to enjoy their meal. I told them that I looked forward to seeing them after the holidays and anticipated their participation in our company's success the following year.

The next working day when I arrived at the office, my first action was to call the employee relations manager into my office.

"There will be no more Christmas parties like that," I told him. "We are a world-class company, and we need to act like it."

Culture change cuts across all actions.

The next year, a few days before Christmas, we closed the shops and offices at noon. We invited all employees to the tastefully-decorated headquarters office building and served hors d'oeuvres, cookies, and punch. We offered them tours of the building. The large, imposing, wooden doors were gone.

People felt valued and included. We got a great reaction from people who now understood the company appreciated their efforts. No more elitism. Everybody was important. They knew they were part of a world-class company.

During the party, I started a conversation with a union official.

"Mr. Gates, what are you doing for Christmas?" he asked.

I told him, "After I have dinner with my wife and daughters, I am leaving Christmas afternoon on a trip to Saudi Arabia. I am going to get an order that we badly need."

He knew our work was slowing down.

The first week in January, I returned to the office with a sixty-eight-million-dollar order. This assured that the plant would keep running full bore. The employees had work.

A few days after we announced the new contract, I received a note in interoffice mail from him. In the

1980s, before email, shop employees within a company communicated using handwritten notes. The union president sent me a message in a personal envelope.

> Mr. Gates,
>
> When I saw you at our Christmas reception and you said you were going to get an order for us, I didn't believe you! I never thought a company president would give up time with his family to work on a holiday. Thank you from all the people in the shop. This order will keep us busy for quite a while.

I cherish that note and still have it. The union president didn't believe that the president of Fuller Company would leave his family on Christmas Day to secure an order in Saudi Arabia. He now knew that real leaders will sacrifice time with their families to do what is necessary for the company and the customer.

Boy, it was quite a turnaround from the days when vice presidents wouldn't leave their offices! From that point forward, the union became a full-fledged member of the team.

This experience also contains another example of the value of integrity in building relationships. As the board of the Saudi Arabian company was negotiating the sixty-eight-million-dollar contract, one member said the general contractor had gone broke building our previous plant for the company. The directors said that Fuller Company would have to guarantee to take over general contracting as a condition of the award in the event that the general contractor failed. The managing director left the board meeting and asked me if I would agree to that condition.

"Sure," I told him.

He returned to the board meeting to report my assurance. The directors asked him to get a letter from me. He told the board that they didn't need a letter.

"If Mr. Gates says he'll stand in their shoes, he will," the managing director told his board.

We were awarded the contract.

As I mentioned earlier, integrity is the most important quality you have as a leader. It is the bedrock of your relationships with all of your stakeholders—your customers, employees, vendors, and the community.

That new attitude of mutual respect stood us in good stead when we took the company private in a leveraged buyout four years later. More on that in the next chapter.

From Fear to Understanding

As you might imagine, there was a lot of fear generated with many employees during the early months of my tenure. For those employees who remained, they had lived through sudden firings. I had laid off people in headquarters doing work that added no value to the company. I had learned at GE, and confirmed at Fuller, that you can lay off around 10 percent of the employees in any organization and improve productivity and customer service. I continue to believe that is true today. In state and federal governments, the number is 20 percent.

By the time I entered the transition phase, the survivors of the early shakeup had seen vice presidents travel to the project sites in foreign countries. They knew that I insisted that all our on-site overseas people understand and respect the culture and practices of host countries, remembering that we are the foreigners. They also heard that they were the president of Fuller Company to the customers in those countries and that the customers will judge our company based on the conduct and performance of the onsite supervisors. Our site supervisors became a significant factor in our customers' impressions of Fuller Company.

Fear is a good short-term motivator, but it isn't a healthy basis for a long-term relationship. As you move from the fix-it to the transition phase, you need to build a culture of trust. Open communication, respect, and trust are the three legs of a strong relationship.

The transition phase is where you get to build all those positive attributes that create a fun workplace and a great customer experience. This is the point where you are turning the corner.

Eliminating Duplication

Early in my tenure, while traveling the world, I studied the organizational chart. I started asking myself, "Why is this being done this way?" Some departments and relationships appeared to make no sense.

As an example, we had two divisions: general products and special products. Each had their own functional engineering departments developing similar products and selling to the same customers. The cost of this duplication is obvious. I scratched my head, wondering about the reasoning behind this particular organizational arrangement.

I discovered that our customers were confused too, particularly when they experienced competition between the two sales forces from one single company— ours! This internal competition was damaging the company's reputation in the marketplace.

Furthermore, these divisions were charging each other for services, which included their respective overhead in the transfer price charged to do business between them. While the extra cost was obvious, it took me some time to understand the rationale for that structure. As an example, if the special projects division sold a project requiring a Fuller Kenyon pump to convey solid-powdered materials, the general projects division would charge the special projects division at list price. These bookkeeping sleights of hand created "funny money" and hurt the customer through the higher cost of our equipment.

At various points in my career, I observed that leaders would develop blocking strategies or create inefficient organizational structures to avoid tasks they did not enjoy. The reasons for this kind of behavior might range from dislike of foreign travel, inability to handle conflict, or any number of reasons that would allow company leaders to avoid disruption of their world. These behaviors amount to abdication of responsibility. I replaced abdication with delegation and accountability.

Inefficiencies were always costly, confusing to customers and creating internal havoc. Whenever I found such blocking strategies or organizational shielding structures to protect leadership, I found that the best course of action was to create clear, customer-focused, results-oriented lines of responsibility.

At Fuller, I created a functional organization with one engineering department, one sales force, and one department for each of the necessary services that supported all units: finance, human resources (HR), and legal. Manufacturing already serviced both divisions, so no reorganization was necessary.

In addition to making customers happier to be doing business with one contact, we also eliminated substantial overhead expenses, a factor in getting to profitability.

Had twenty-first century communication and information technology been available in the 1980s, I would have been able to make another important reduction in overhead by eliminating the preparation of reports to corporate headquarters. We would have benefitted from some of the real-time data and communications software available today, allowing sales reports, manufacturing, and distribution data to be online all the time. Instead, we incurred unavoidable overhead by generating hard-copy reports due to the era in which we operated. I was still able to make modest reductions in this cost with the technology available at the time.

I questioned why each report was necessary and assessed the effect if it were eliminated. Reports have limited usefulness. They tell you what happened in the past. You can learn from them when you study these records of the past.

We determined if a specific report indeed had value. Then I decided whether the frequency of the submission could be lengthened (such as quarterly instead of monthly) and if we could make a reduction in the number of people receiving reports. By drastically reducing the number of reports generated by staff, I was able to eliminate useless work. Within a year, we had streamlined lines of reporting and the amount of reporting that was required to operate effectively.

Even with today's technology, these are great questions to ask on a frequent basis in any organization. If you are truly dedicated to operating a business that serves customers and delivers valuable products and services in a cost-effective way, examine the productivity of your employees. Your employees may be busy, but that is a very different thing from being productive. Ask yourself: What does this employee produce? Does it add value to the business? Does it advance the profitability of the business? Alternately, does it impede customer service? Is it a drain on company resources, adding no value? In other words, drill deep in the organization. Ignoring the little things leads to mediocrity.

Transitioning Leadership Styles

Intense scrutiny and rapid decision-making were instrumental in changing the culture from one of comfort and excuses to one of outstanding customer service, action, and accountability. It didn't happen overnight, but it didn't take that long either. Within a year, we had streamlined the organization to its essential functions, connected with customers, and torn down walls between the executive suite and the employees, both literally and figuratively.

The timing of transitioning to each successive leadership style is crucial. It requires a balance between meeting the schedule to complete the turnaround and ensuring that the organization has reacted appropriately to each preceding leadership style during the transition. Knowing when and how to transition to the next leadership style will depend on the turnaround leader's personality, style, and experience.

Your leadership style is how you accomplish the tasks you own.

Your personal leadership style is unique to you. There is no right or wrong to your personal style, only differences among people. Just like in all other areas of

---

your life, don't try to copy another person's leadership style. It won't work. Refine your own style.

The difficulty or ease of each transition also depends on the recognition, acceptance, and support generated within the ranks of the employees during each phase. There is risk at each phase, but in all decisions, leaders take risks!

A successful turnaround will hone your leadership skills by utilizing these three different leadership styles in a short period of time—autocratic, transitional, and empowering. You will get a chance to learn the attributes of each one during a trial by fire while creating a successful business out of a failed enterprise.

While the leader is cycling through different leadership styles to facilitate the turnaround, it is critical that the U-turn leader define the new culture appropriate to the organization going forward.

As you move from being autocratic to transitional to empowering, you will need to make sure employees are with you each step of the way. How? Keep everybody informed; be open and transparent.

Honest, Two-Way Communication

Destroying the culture was easy. Building and maintaining a new one during the transition was hard work. The CEO is essential to a successful effort because he or she sets the tone for the entire organization. Be prepared to work even harder than before; your hard work *will* be rewarded. A successful cultural transformation is truly a professional development reward.

The old adage that communication is a two-way street is never truer than when you are affecting a turnaround. Another old cliché applies here as well: the words "listen" and "silent" are spelled with the same letters; in order to listen, one must be silent. Particularly during the early stages of the transition phase, listening will be important because there will be a few employees who are hostile to the changes. They will preach to anyone who will listen about how the new actions are wrong, unnccessary, and selfish.

Since you will be establishing the new culture with every word and every deed, make sure the culture is clearly defined so that you are sending a consistent message. To be effective, that message needs to be communicated regularly—both formally and informally—orally and in writing. The new culture must be clear in every move, decision, and action, and it must be consistent with the desired outcome. Remember, you are being scrutinized, and not everyone is your friend.

Not only must U-turn leaders be consistent in their communications, but their actions must absolutely support and embrace the culture they building as well. Any messages that aren't consistent with the new culture must be eliminated.

I also continued to spend a lot of time practicing MBWA (Management By Walking Around). Some of the employees were frightened when I stopped at their drawing boards (computers weren't in common use yet) and asked what they were working on. Part of it was because of the reputation I had earned during the fix-it phase and another part of their reaction was due to the fact that the president had never been seen up close and personal before. You learn a lot on those visits. I would ask which project they were working on. Many wouldn't know!

There was no connection between a majority of the employees and the customer. This was particularly true with our shop workers in our factories. In the minds of the workers, they were doing a job in isolation. They had no connection to the big picture, our product, or our customers.

Connecting Employees to Customers

One day, I was making a presentation at the Manheim, Pennsylvania factory to the shop workers about a new program we were launching—Fuller Follow Through. One man, who was an officer of an international union, was somewhat combative. Rather than challenge him, which came naturally to me, I decided to engage him.

"I like your aggressiveness," I told him. "I think you would be a good salesman for the company. I'm going to take you with me to our next monthly project-review meeting at the customer's site. You're going to Mexico," I told him.

I'm sure he didn't believe me, but a few days before the next meeting in Hermosillo, Mexico, I called him on the phone.

"Get ready to go to Mexico next week," I told him. "I will send a car to pick you up on Sunday night. It will take you a motel nearby so we can leave early in the morning to catch a plane to Tucson."

His stunned "Yes, Mr. Gates" had none of the combativeness of his earlier talk on the factory floor.

The following week, our driver picked us up and took us to the airport. I greeted him in a hearty manner. He was pleasant and polite, but I sensed some uneasiness.

Just prior to getting on the plane, he said, "I'd better go to the bathroom because it's a long flight."

I knew then for certain that my instinct was correct. He had never flown before. He didn't know there were bathrooms on the plane. We had a pleasant plane ride. We arrived at the Tucson airport, rented a car, and drove ninety to one-hundred miles per hour toward Mexico.

We arrived at the customer's plant and were hosted at a dinner that night. At dinner, the customer CEO asked me how the manufacturing of the equipment was going.

I turned to my employee.

"Go ahead and tell him," I prompted.

Without any advance warning or coaching, he said, "It's Mr. Gates' and others' jobs to get the orders. We will make sure that we build the equipment to our quality standards, and we'll ship it on time!"

He made me proud. What a risk but what a payoff! The customer was delighted, and this union worker became a happy and loud cheerleader for the company! The next day, we toured the plant, and for the first time *ever*, he understood the importance of the work he performed. He saw it for himself. He even bought his wife a gift.

That experience led me to arrange tours for our employees of local cement plants that used our equipment. Initially, I made trips to local cement plants and took employees with me so that they could see our products in action. After all, I had found that there was no connection between the customers and the employees. The best way to connect our employees to our customers was to make field trips so that the people who designing and building our products had a clear vision of how it operated in our customers' plants.

More Customer Connections

I saw the tremendous impact these customer visits had on the performance of employees. When they could see our products in action, they had a new enthusiasm and spark in their attitudes. When employees came back from both domestic and foreign trips, they became "coffee-machine leaders," but the kind who were on my side. I continued the practice.

We had a global-service division. One female employee scheduled the numerous service engineers and technicians to locations around the world, making their many visa and transportation arrangements. She was efficient and courteous, an excellent employee.

She had not traveled to any foreign country, yet she was communicating daily with offices there. I invited her to accompany her manager on a trip to Pakistan, a strict Muslim country. In that country, there were rules governing the dress and conduct of women. She was briefed on the customs, made the trip, and proved to be an excellent ambassador while there. When she returned, she was an even better employee. She learned that she performed a very important step in our ability to satisfy our many international customers.

I made another such investment in another employee because these trips had proven worthwhile to morale and customer service. A young man in our shipping department arranged transportation for our products to destinations all around the world. I had been invited to the dedication of a plant we had built in Turkey, so I asked him if he would like to accompany me. He was delighted to go.

We arrived at our destination, a five-star hotel on the Black Sea coast at the customer's expense. The accommodations were lavish. We retired to our rooms. I had a very nice suite, and he had a somewhat lesser, but still quite wonderful, room. The next morning, we met at the restaurant for breakfast. We had a myriad of selections. I expected that he would be impressed with the quality of our accommodations. Our accommodations were first class! I was surprised.

Over breakfast, his first words to me were not, "Wow, what a place!" Instead, he looked at me wide-eyed and said, "Wow, what a culture shock!" That told me a lot. It confirmed for me the value of this kind of exposure to employees like him who were important to the organization. He was able to see the result of his work and, particularly, the importance of their work. No longer were the destinations on his bills of lading just funny names in faraway places. They were operating plants all over a big and interesting world.

We continued this practice and built professional pride and commitment.

Ongoing Cultural Changes

Even while there were major organizational and operational changes going on, some remnants of the ruling-class culture in the company remained. For example, corporate officers flew first class, and all others flew coach. First class is a luxury that most business people who travel don't need.

This was brought home to me when a Far East sales manager and I traveled from one location to another in the South Pacific. He was the face of the company to all our customers in that part of the world, yet he was in the rear of the airplane with peanuts, coke, and a cafeteria-style meal. Meanwhile, I was offered premium drinks of all types (which I declined because I don't drink) and feasted on lobster, caviar, and bananas Foster in the front cabin. Sitting in my large leather seat, I was actually embarrassed that I was traveling in such style while the local executive, who represented Fuller Company to the customer, flew coach.

Upon landing, I told our Far East representative, "That's the last time you will fly coach. From now on, all of us will fly business class."

That policy went into effect immediately, with the only caveat that when traveling overnight, all employees were expected to go to work when arriving at their destination.

Two beliefs guided me in this and other turnaround successes. The first is that you can't cost-reduce your way to prosperity. The second is that there is a time to save money and a time to spend money. It's important to know when and how to flip the switch. This was the time to spend money.

※

That particular change completed this transition period. Employees knew they were respected for the jobs they did and how well they represented the company. It was a great morale booster. It also improved customer relations and productivity.

As you might imagine, a couple of hotshots tried to beat the system and ordered business-class tickets for a trip to Canada. Shortly upon their return, they were ex-employees. That sent the message that employees were being treated like they were working for a world-class company because they were working hard, but that didn't mean that things had returned to the old days. Slackers were not part of the new company culture.

Lasting Feelings

During this transition, most employees became willing and productive partners, and they understood the changes I made. However, some whom I had treated harshly or unfairly in their view had negative attitudes and still do today, I'm sure.

This transition period lasted for more than a year. During this time, it was obvious within the company and to our competition that we were becoming a global force to be reckoned with. We were gaining market share and were increasingly profitable. Our employees enjoyed winning, and they reaped the rewards that went with our success.

We became a global leader. Our competition was losing market share and could not understand why. An oversimplification is that we employed a relationship strategy. Most of our competitors employed a transaction strategy. In other words, at every level of leadership, we developed a respect for relationships with our customers. For instance, I knew the plant managers and maintenance supervisors (they buy spare parts, remember?) as well as I knew the CEOs of all our customers.

Our competitors generally invested in visiting customers only when there was a major project in the planning process. If an existing plant was to be expanded or modified, or a new plant being considered, our competitors swarmed around the customer. However, we visited on a regular basis and had a good knowledge of the status of projects at all times.

Betting on Myself

When I was hired at Fuller Company, I was offered the opportunity for a flat salary or I could take twenty-thousand dollars less in salary and have the opportunity for a bonus. I took the bonus option. I knew myself better than they did, and besides, I was getting used to taking calculated risks. My early, gut assessment said, "Take the bonus."

I earned the bonus based on the improved performance of the company and, more importantly, so did the vice presidents, which was a first for them. To show their appreciation, the vice presidents presented me with a shotgun. I was a trap shooter, and the gift was thoughtful and somewhat personal. Because I took that calculated risk and created value for the leaders around me, I gained credibility among my peers. They saw that my leadership style was working and making a positive impact on the business. I had earned their respect by making hard choices; now I was getting love from most of them because they were benefitting.

It was time for all of us at Fuller Company to start reaping the rewards of our hard work.

Chapter 7: Takeaways

1. Change is happening, but don't relax.
2. Help people understand the importance of their work. Connect them directly with the customer.
3. Know your customers and maintain regular contact with them.
4. Keep communicating and keep listening.
5. Eliminate functional silos.
6. Solidify the culture.
7. Celebrate successes. Involve people.
8. Success is hard work.

Chapter 8

Stage Three: The Growth and Success Phase

When things go well, resist the urge to relax. Adding cost is easier than reducing cost.

After four years, the company was on its way to grow from a mere 3 percent of market share to approximately 25 percent of market share in our served market. At this time, GATX made a decision to exit all of their manufacturing businesses. I and four vice presidents decided to make a bid to buy Fuller Company from GATX and take it private. We had to compete with several outside groups, but our edge was our in-depth knowledge of the company. It was a risk but a measured one because of this knowledge.

Our competition began to spread rumors that our buyout position wasn't viable— after all, we lacked financial viability. It was in the interest of our competitors to point out our weaknesses. One of our perceived weaknesses was the fact that we were a union shop and had to renegotiate our union contract. We could be subject to a strike, and our customers were vulnerable to possible late delivery of their equipment.

However, I had established credibility and a strong relationship with our union leadership.

I went to one of the leaders and told him the issue.

"Our competitors are saying we can't deliver on our promises because we are vulnerable to a strike. You and I are on the same team here. Our competitors are the enemy. Can you work with me?"

Union leadership knew I was good for my word. "Yes, Elmer. We will help you get where you need to go," he said.

I drew on the good will I had created. Our factory workers appreciated being included in trips to local cement plants and being invited to our Christmas party. They remembered my Christmas trip to Saudi Arabia when I brought home the sixty-eight-million-dollar contract that kept our manufacturing line rolling. By those and other consistent actions over time, we were able to negotiate a five-year union contract.

When competitors and naysayers put out the word that our buyout was on thin ice, I was able to step forward and present a five-year, locked-in union contract, showing our customers and competitors that Fuller Company was positioned to deliver on its promises for the next half decade.

We eliminated the strike threat as an issue with our customers. We now owned the company.

Beyond the Turnaround—Maintaining Success

As the company begins to realize the benefit of the previous two phases, it is your job to identify new challenges for the company.

Maintaining a company culture requires the same attention to detail as during the transition while it is being built. The CEO retains the responsibility. In all cases, culture is the responsibility of leadership; he or she owns it. I've seen too many times when this important activity was relegated to the human-resources function. This is always a mistake. Human resources is a valuable organization and administrative function, but it has no real power to shape culture in the eyes of employees. The CEO, on the other hand, wields authority, and his or her presence has impact. You can't delegate that kind of power or responsibility.

I call this phase the growth-and-success phase. After establishing a culture of "reject the status quo" and "we can do better," with a laser focus on the customer, you can be confident that you will prosper by maintaining the culture.

In this phase, which you hope will last forever, it is extremely important for all employees to maintain a sharp external focus. Know your markets, know your competition, know the rapidly changing technology, and focus on how it can improve every aspect of your business. Teach and preach execution; plans are only valuable when they are implemented.

Getting the Job Descriptions Right

As volume builds, managers are inclined to want to add people and to relax. Resist that temptation. Build a lean attitude into the culture. When an opening occurs, never replace in kind. Evaluate changes in the market, in technology, and in the workload of each person in the organization. In other words, do an organizational analysis. Costs are much easier to build into an organization than to take out.

Don't use existing job descriptions; instead, create statements of expectation that focus on the future.

In our rapidly changing business and technological environment, job responsibilities can change frequently. Job descriptions must change with them. To respond, written statements of expectations set the stage for employees to do what is necessary to help them advance the company.

Because position descriptions are a list of tasks, they are usually ignored by the employee and their boss, except once a year at appraisal time. That is why expectations are far superior to job descriptions. Used appropriately, a list of expectations promotes more frequent communication between the leader and his or her people. After all, employees are widely proclaimed as a company's most precious asset, so why not engage them frequently to make sure they are able to respond to conditions? The best use of your human-resource asset is to make sure you are coaching your employees to excellence rather than appraising them against a list of tasks during the review cycle. The word "appraising" sounds punitive to many employees, while the word "coaching" has positive connotations.

That leads us to a discussion of the problem with performance appraisals. The person getting the appraisal is usually nervous, and all he or she cares about is the percentage of a raise he or she will get for the upcoming year. His or her mind isn't on the performance appraisal, and his or her boss is not anxious to deliver it either. I found that most bosses I've asked tell me they are reluctant to give their employees an honest evaluation. This makes the process unproductive. However, if you use the time to coach an employee, that is a positive experience for both of you, and it takes the spotlight off the dreaded "appraisal." A coaching session takes the discussion from what the employee has done right or wrong in the past and places the emphasis on how the boss and the employee can work together to improve the business in the future.

How do I know the boss is not anxious to deliver an honest appraisal? Because I've surveyed my classes and seminar participants, that's why. In my leadership seminars, which I have given to hundreds of attendees, I ask bosses to use the 4-X-100-percent test regarding the employee's annual review. I ask them

1. Have you been 100 percent honest
2. with 100 percent of your employees

3. 100 percent of the time
4. in 100 percent of their appraisals?

Only one leader has ever answered yes, and I believed him! I think it is that rare. This begs the question: are performance appraisals a positive or a negative event for employees in your company? I think the answer lies in the fact the employee isn't even getting real information.

Stop appraising. Start coaching.

More on Employee Expectations

If "appraisals" are a backward-looking and unproductive activity, their corollary is the written job description. Instead, I have found that statements of expectation are superior to job descriptions. Job descriptions, by definition, are static. They describe the past. On the other hand, statements of expectations, by their nature, change as the environment changes.

As you saw from several positions I assumed at GE and the position at Fuller, I got hired into job descriptions that were several years old. My performance was measured against outdated, and in some cases incorrect information. Perhaps that was okay forty or fifty years ago because the pace of change was very slow. Today, if you have a job description that was written five years ago, you might as well have nothing at all. So many things changed during that time, particularly in this era of technology.

Instead, a statement of expectations describes specific tasks to be accomplished in order to meet the overall objective, and it is a more meaningful document.

A statement of expectation encourages leaders and employees to coach and be coached on the spot. You receive more frontline feedback regarding employee performance at the same time. With this ongoing feedback and coaching loop, there are no surprises during the annual review. The annual appraisal then becomes a session to review employee performance with an eye toward coaching to continued excellence.

It is time to lose the dreaded annual performance appraisal and salary adjustment, which is painful for the employee and the boss.

Leading into the Future

As you fine-tune your culture of growth and success, your leadership style evolves into one where you encourage the ownership mentality of your employees. Taken to its logical conclusion, you are encouraging your most innovative employees to assume more and bigger responsibilities in your organization.

The final and most enduring leadership style is the entrepreneurial style, one where you are building and leading an organization of entrepreneurial leaders and entrepreneurial employees. This third phase of leadership should usher in an era of real results and opportunities, while each level of leadership is freed up to having more "thinking" time and less "doing" time.

As the company begins to realize the benefits of the implementation of the turnaround principles, it is your job to identify new challenges for the company.

At different levels, in any place in the organization, your turnaround job follows the same steps:

1. Destroy the existing culture.
2. Determine the right culture for the organization.
3. Build and maintain the new culture.
4. Develop continuing new challenges.

At this point in the Fuller Company turnaround, we had reached the fourth step.

Empowerment

It is now time to empower employees to make more decisions. The closer you drive decision-making into the ranks, the faster and, in most cases, the better decisions will be made. Empowerment is based on trust, training, and teamwork— all hallmarks of your new culture. Before empowering an employee, you have to be clear on the decision you are delegating. You have to give him or her the authority to make decisions, and then you need to stand behind him or her when he or she does.

The boss's attitude needs to be, "I put you in charge. I am responsible for training you, coaching you, and making sure you are capable of the responsibility I have given you."

Before letting go of the reins, ask the person if he or she feels properly trained to make the decisions you are giving him or her the responsibility to make. If not, provide more training. As part of the gradual transfer of responsibility and authority, explain that any mistake is a joint mistake shared by both of you. You will both consider any mistakes tuition, with the expectation that you also both will learn from any errors. Trust is critical in order for this to be effective. If the first time the employee makes a mistake, he or she has negative consequences, then your efforts at empowerment will be dead.

Any empowered organization with responsibility and authority pushed out toward the edges can be a lean organization if properly led.

Again, it cannot be emphasized enough that coaching, training, communication, and trust are critical for empowerment to work.

Building a Culture of Innovation

For a company to grow and prosper, it has to be looking toward the future. At Fuller Company, even though we had made good progress in building our culture of responsibility, the company still lacked creativity. I told the organization that I had established a 250,000-dollar innovation fund. The money would go to anyone with an idea to improve a product, substitute a product, or design a new part. The only requirement was that he or she explain it to me so I could understand it. At first, there was skepticism, but after a slow start, we started getting a flow of ideas and some patent applications.

With some trepidation, one entrepreneurial employee presented me with the idea to reduce the cost and extend the life of a consumable part of one piece of equipment. He knew a lot more than I did about this process, but it was a new idea, and I approved it. He was surprised but empowered. A few years later, we started a program to honor those who had submitted patents, including this man. After we sold the company, this particular employee started his own company and did extremely well. It was a two-fer. Fuller Company profited from the creativity program, and it gave him the impetus to start his own company.

The innovation mind-set is even more critical to future survival today than it was in 1985. Fifty years ago, the life cycle of products was very long. Today, the life cycle of products is very short. Technology has created an environment of continuous product development. That calls for continuous, honest, two-way communication where the boss and employee are constantly examining what is going on in the organization, asking what is changing in the industry, and examining how things can be done better. It gets back to the first lesson I learned in my career: never accept the status quo. In that spirit, encourage innovation in your new culture.

Elmer D. Gates

The challenge in the grow-and-prosper phase is to build and maintain a culture of success, customer service, innovation, and teamwork. Nobody relaxes. The CEO still sets and leads the maintenance of the culture. It is a difficult but essential task of the CEO and the functional business unit leaders to maintain the new culture. It requires ongoing vigilance embraced by all company management using all the principles of U-Turn Leadership.

At this stage, there is a risk of the start of the deterioration of the culture because some people will want to get comfortable. Remember, success is hard work. If you run your business like you are in a turnaround situation, you will never find yourself in a turnaround situation.

When you reach the grow-and-prosper stage, you run the risk of an entitlement culture taking hold, as people want to relax and enjoy the fruits of their labor.

By the time it was obvious that we were definitely in the grow-and-prosper phase, one of my vice presidents came into my office. I welcomed him, and after some small talk, he launched into the purpose of his visit.

"Boss, you have done a great job in fixing the business," he said, setting the stage for his request.

"Thank you. All of our hard work is paying off, and now we've got to keep it up," I said.

"The other officers feel the same way I do. We've been thinking. We think it is time you should have a better company car. You should drive a Cadillac," he said.

I drove an Oldsmobile '98, a great General Motors car. In the General Motors product line, it was next to the top of the heap. The Cadillac was their premier line, so by purchasing Oldsmobiles, we were one step away from the top without the panache—and price—of the premium product. The vice presidents drove Olds '88s, one step down from mine. In the General Motors line, while Cadillac is the premium product, the Chevrolet (or "Chevy") is its entry-level model. In the mid-twentieth century, General Motors was synonymous with corporate America, and its products were part of the cultural reference. Well-made products are compared to "the Cadillac" and cheaper products are compared to "the Chevy."

I studied him and considered his request for a second.

"Let's discuss this," I said. "If I drive into a customer's plant in a Cadillac, what is their first thought?" I didn't wait for him to answer. I responded to my own question. "They will think we are charging too much for our products. So the answer is thanks, but I'll keep the Olds."

I saw through the real reason for his visit. He and the other officers all drove Olds '88 company cars, and they wanted Olds '98 cars. They reasoned if they could move me into a Cadillac, everybody would be upgraded to a better car. Imagine the cost of such a decision! This discussion wasn't about me and what I had done. It was about them wanting to relax and play the role of the hotshot at the company's expense.

The next time that individual was due for a new car, he received a Chevrolet. At our next staff meeting, I related the story and reminded all the officers our job was far from done. There were more orders to get; more global projects to execute better, faster, and cheaper; and more improvements to be made in customer service, quality, and productivity. More costs still needed to be taken out of the business. It was no time to rest and relax. It was time to lead by example.

At times like these, company cultures can quickly be destroyed by one frivolous decision.

More about the Destruction of Company Cultures

I've been involved in two mergers; in the first, we sold the Fuller Company to a competitor and in the other, a bank in which I was involved merged with another. In both cases, the acquiring organization dismantled years of hard-won culture building almost immediately after the deal went through.

In the Fuller Company merger, Fuller was known for its outstanding customer service. Our competitor, F. L. Smidth, to which we sold Fuller, was known for having the best technology and R&D. The acquiring technology company, F. L.Smidth, had a transaction strategy in which it paid close attention to the large projects that were being let, minimizing other potential customer contact. Fuller's relationship strategy meant that we were courting the whole potential customer base, always building a relationship for the next opportunity. The marriage was a natural one, blending the two strengths.

Here is an example of those two strategies.

During my tenure at the head of Fuller, I had a good and friendly relationship with the Chairman of F. L. Smidth. We occasionally met and socialized when he was in the United States. During one trip, I met him in New York City for lunch. A cement company in Hermosillo, Mexico, put out a request for proposals for a new plant. We had bid on it, but F. L. Smidth was still debating whether to submit a proposal.

"So, Elmer, do you think that Hermosillo job is going to go?" he asked me.

He did not know that I already had a letter of intent from the customer in my back pocket saying they planned to give Fuller the order.

"Yes, I think it will go," I told him, not letting him know the deal was done. "Since I'm not a drinking man, I'll bet you a bottle of scotch for a bottle of Aquavit."

He made good on the bottle of Aquavit.

You can have a relationship strategy or you can have a transaction strategy, and you can't meld those two. They are mutually exclusive.

Because of our focus on the customer, Fuller was known for its relationship strategy within the first year after I arrived.

For a while, I made the mistake of thinking that we could be number one in technology too. I soon came to the realization that customers want you to deliver the technology, not necessarily to develop it. So, I reasoned, if I can deliver the technology by licensing or acquiring it in some way, I don't need to put that money into R&D. When F. L. Smidth finally bought us, we were merging the best customer-service company in the world with the best technology company in the world. Within a month after they acquired us, they changed the whole culture.

After Fuller was sold to F. L. Smidth, the transaction strategy was imposed on the new acquisition, and Fuller's results were never the same. What took years to build was gone in a few weeks. I learned a lesson watching Fuller's culture be dismantled almost overnight. When the new leadership's priorities changed, the culture changed very rapidly.

The second situation was a bank acquisition in which I was a shareholder and director of the acquired bank. The buying bank was losing share to us, again due to a significant difference in approach to customers. After the acquisition, the buyer told our former employees to forget everything they had learned at the old bank about customer service and do it the new bank's way. I observed the phenomenon again. Cultures take time to build; they can be destroyed in a week. More about the bank in the next section.

Manage Government Relations Too

Building relationships with one or more levels of government is an important part of your relationship strategy and is critical for organizations doing business internationally. At Fuller, we built strong connections with our government representatives, and we used those relationships in 1990 to win an important order.

I led a small number of sales and engineering people to Indonesia to negotiate for a large-capacity cement plant. It would be our first project there. After a week of intense negotiations, we received a letter of intent for the plant. Before returning to Bethlehem, we celebrated briefly and then went home to get to work.

About a week later, I received a fax saying that the customer had decided to award the contract to a German competitor. We suspected that someone had "influenced" a company executive, an Indonesian government official or both—a quite common practice in some countries.

I spent a few seconds considering our hard-won award. Then I decided, "Like hell they are going to steal this order from us."

My first call was to our congressman, asking him to call the US ambassador in Jakarta and also asking him to meet with the country leadership to discuss our case. The Indonesian government was heavily involved in private-sector businesses and remains so to this day.

I told our congressman, "Prior to his meeting, our ambassador should have a summary of all the sorts of aid that the United States gives to Indonesia. Compile the same information for Germany. Share those lists with them."

I asked that, in parallel, our congressman ask the US commercial attaché to meet with the Indonesian cement company officials and share this information with them as well.

Finally, I requested a personal meeting with our ambassador.

These specific and targeted actions announced to the customer and to the Indonesian prime minister that not only Fuller Company, but the US government as well, had an interest in this contract.

On the heels of these actions by the United States government on our behalf, our team rushed back to Jakarta. After one friendly negotiating session with the customer, we secured the order.

The US ambassador and commercial attaché won this order for us.

Following the successful rescue of this contract by the quick and decisive actions of our advocates, I met with the ambassador and the commercial attaché to thank them on behalf of all the people at Fuller Company. Fuller's relationships with our federal officials paid off handsomely for us. This particular contract led to almost a billion dollars of orders in Indonesia— quite a return on our investment in maintaining strong government relations.

Another Day, Another Management Strategy

In this book, you find me discussing what has been coined as a "lean" approach to management. I need to take some time to explain. When I was disrupting cultures and implementing new management techniques in the '60s, '70s and '80s, the term "lean" did not exist. I was just doing what made good sense to streamline the organization, install good practices and processes, focus on the customer, and eliminate waste. Today, those are the hallmarks of a lean culture.

It is a good time to mention this because as you further reinforce the new culture, you won't need to periodically introduce programs as "continuous improvement," or "journey to excellence," or "six sigma" because you are instilling a new and lasting culture in the organization that is innovative and always looks to do better. Typically, after a certain amount of time, these improvement programs die an unceremonious death, and the culture of the organization has not been permanently changed.

Employees often appropriately complain about the institution of new management-improvement programs as the "flavor of the month." A true, continuous improvement program is one that is engrained in the culture, not imposed by an outside organization or consultant. It is led by the CEO. You don't need to put a label on good, common-sense management practices.

Furthermore, if a new management practice is implemented, it must come from the top, whether that is the CEO or the head of a functional business unit. The leader has power and authority he or she cannot lend to anyone else, including an outside consulting firm.

Look Outward

As you develop your company as a thriving enterprise within your community, you turn your focus outside the company walls to supporting local activities.

I attended community meetings and political events with other heads of other local corporations. At one such meeting with our congressman, he told local business leaders that the strong dollar hurt American business because our country's products were more expensive compared to our international competitors.

I stood up and disagreed strongly.

"The strong dollar won't affect Fuller Company," I told the attendees. "We will grow our international markets and will do it successfully! We will use quality, performance, and delivery as well as price to win the business."

My positive mind-set would not be deterred by negative talk, either inside our company or in the larger business community. We were part of the local and national business environments, and I took our place at the table to advocate for global competitiveness.

Community Service

The most important community service a CEO can provide is to run a long-term successful company. By doing so, the company will have discretionary income to support the community. The employees will have discretionary income to use to support community organizations, and they will have time to volunteer.

Beyond the local business environment, successful CEOs understand there is a significant infrastructure available to their employees and their families, including educational, recreational, and cultural activities.

Encourage volunteerism! You have strengthened the company, provided good, dependable jobs for families, and now your employees can contribute by spreading your influence throughout the community.

Reflections on Fuller

To accomplish the transformation of a failing company to a world leader required hard work every day. To maintain a successful world-class operation is even harder. Some people want to relax, and others think that maintaining close contact with the customer is not as important as it was earlier in the turnaround. Still others lose their sense of urgency and even their sense of purpose.

It is your job as the turnaround leader to bring new challenges and reinforce the creativity culture you have developed while still rewarding outstanding performers as appropriate. Thinking is hard. Continued success requires more thinking and less doing.

Good luck in your continuing turnaround leadership!

Chapter 8: Takeaways

1. Delegate but don't abdicate responsibility. Hold individuals accountable for results.
2. Conduct two-way communications often. Be a patient listener.
3. Give meaning to every employee's work.
4. Use statements of expectations instead of job descriptions that emphasize outcomes, not tasks. Look forward, not backward.
5. Instill that the time to be a hero is when you have done it, not before! Results matter. Intentions? Not so much!
6. Continually identify new challenges for the company. Don't relax! There is still a lot of work to do.
7. The hardest business to run is a successful one.
8. Maintain contact with your customers, employees, and other stakeholders.
9. Reinforce the culture.
10. Don't relax!

Part 3

Lessons for a Turnaround World

Part 3: Lessons for a Turnaround World

Introduction

Every business can use U-Turn Leadership principles because every business presents an opportunity for improvement and growth. It doesn't matter if your business is a start-up in a business incubator or if your company is just stagnating in your marketplace with little growth. In this section, we will discuss U-Turn Leadership principles in action, both in a start-up services industry and a declining industry in the rust belt.

After my success with, and then sale of, Fuller Company, I was in a position to turn my attention to building a business from the ground up, using what I had learned in all my turnaround experiences.

First, I was invited to be on the board of a new local bank. Having grown up in a small community, I appreciated the warmth of a community bank. It was a great chance to influence management and customer relations and build a new successful community bank.

The last chapter is a special case that is close to me. Bethlehem, Pennsylvania, was the headquarters of the Bethlehem Steel Company. Bethlehem Steel was one of the giants of American industry beginning in the '30s and through the '70s. By the time I arrived in Bethlehem in 1982, it was already in decline.

As a member of the local business community, I met and got to know the last three presidents of "the Steel," as it was known to the locals. Through those relationships, I developed a position from which to intimately observe its demise. Since this book is about U-Turn Leadership, "the Steel" deserves attention as the final chapter to the book because it so clearly demonstrates a company desperately in need of a turnaround and the deterioration that occurs when these principles of U-Turn Leadership are ignored.

Join me for this last section, where we find out how to build a business from the ground up based on U-Turn Leadership principles and then what an organization looks like that is beyond recovery.

Chapter 9

Lessons for Startups

After selling Fuller Company to a competitor and serving as a consultant for a period of time, I officially retired. My success at Fuller positioned me to be able to take on roles in the community where I could continue to contribute in new ways.

I was approached to be a director of a local bank, Ambassador. We had built Ambassador into a successful bank with a strong relationship strategy. We trained our people to be customer-relations employees. For example, we didn't have traditional tellers as the banking industry defines those positions. They were personal banker positions.

In 1999, Ambassador was approached by Fulton Bank, seeking to merge. I wanted to see Ambassador remain independent and was not in favor of the merger. I lost that battle and was the sole dissenting vote in the sale. On the day the transaction was final, I told the board that at the right time, I would start another bank.

When Ambassador sold to Fulton, Ambassador's customer-centric culture was quickly destroyed. The culture that had built Ambassador was gone in a month because the acquiring company went back to traditional tellers and other common banking practices.

It was interesting to observe. Not once did Fulton executives question how we achieved the success that made us a desirable acquisition. They didn't ask about our unique use of personal bankers rather than tellers. They immediately concluded that we were paying our employees too much rather than look at our total compensation for redefining those positions and giving our personal bankers more responsibility. They would have learned that our total compensation was less than theirs.

During the Ambassador Bank years, Executive Vice President David Lobach, an experienced and entrepreneurial banker, and I had developed a strong relationship. We saw eye to eye. After Ambassador was sold and his non-compete clause expired, David and I repaired to a restaurant at a country inn, away from the prying eyes of community leaders, and on the back of a napkin we drew plans for our new bank.

We developed and documented the vision for the bank and confirmed that building and maintaining a culture would be our key to success.

We agreed. "We are going to run lean, we are going to hire great people, treat them great, treat our customers great, and great things will happen."

"And we are going to have fun doing it," Dave said. "Fun, family, and whatever it takes." That was, and is, our motto.

In 2001, David and I opened Embassy Bank in a construction trailer in a hotel parking lot. We employed the culture we each had embraced during our career experiences—mine in manufacturing coupled with David's entrepreneurial banking success. We emphasized to our team that if we a) hired great people, b) treated them great, and c) took great care of our customers, great things would happen. We were right. They did and still are.

Under David's leadership as chairman and CEO, Embassy Bank has enjoyed thirteen years of double-digit growth, even as the national and global economy suffered. Similar to the comment I made to the congressman several years earlier, David said during the economic downturn in 2008, "We will not participate in this recession." Interpreted, that means, "no excuses." Our expectations are that we will sustain our growth.

The experience we had with Ambassador Bank gave us the confidence to know that if we took that model and enhanced it, we could build another successful bank.

We built Embassy Bank on a few strong pillars:

1. Reject the status quo.
2. Never be satisfied.
3. We can always do better.
4. Great people will ensure business success.
5. The customer comes first and is the reason we are here.

We also agreed that we would not attend banking conferences. Too many executives accept that many of their competitors are smarter than they are and attend conferences to learn what others are doing. While we weren't arrogant about it, we felt that our model was sufficiently different from our competitors, which made the value of our attendance questionable. As an example, a whole lot of banks were convinced that subprime lending was an opportunity. We didn't. A lot of banks sustained substantial losses, and we did not.

Embassy Bank stands as confirmation that the same practices that are employed in a turnaround also work in a start-up. The only difference is that in a start-up, you are not fixing the business; you are utilizing the lessons learned in previous situations to prevent problems and building a successful business from the ground up.

Best Practices at Embassy Bank

Embassy Bank runs lean. People are trained and cross-trained. Employees are empowered. They have authority and responsibility. They are paid very well compared to their peers in other banks to take responsibility and action. We also treat mistakes as an opportunity to learn together; we call it tuition. We look at every learning opportunity as a joint opportunity for the employee and his or her boss to learn. As a result, every person who works at Embassy is better equipped to not only work in the banking industry, but they have learned enough basic principles about running a business that they could be successful in any number of industries.

In a start-up culture, you hire the people with the winning attitudes that you need to build your business from the time the starting gun is fired. You hire for attitude and integrity and then train for aptitude. In my experience, pretesting is not helpful in the hiring process. It is form over substance. Emotional intelligence and other personality tests don't give you the information that you need to hire well. At one point, the bank hired a consultant who used a type of personality test for her approach to hiring. She took credit for our success. I said, "Here's the reason for our success," and put my hand on David's shoulder. We have grown our own hiring style.

The best way to hire the best people is to talk to them and get to know them. Before we hire at Embassy, applicants meet a lot of people. We are looking to see if they are outgoing, if they are comfortable with who they are, if they like people, and if they are flexible. We need people who get along easily with others. After all, they need to get along with us! And then, of course, they need to like working with customers. Next, their flexibility shows us that they won't say, "That's not my job."

We also focus on maximizing a person's strengths. If one of our employees is having a difficulty, we find a position that will better utilize his or her strengths. And interestingly, on those very rare occasions when an individual cannot adjust to our culture, they tend to self-select and leave. However, given the opportunity, most employees move to the new position and excel.

They have to be people who want to learn and improve. Given that kind of raw material, we can develop exceptional employees. And we have. This approach to employee hiring and development has led Embassy Bank to our thirteen years of double-digit growth with very low employee turnover.

Hiring mistakes happen. You can inherit them or you can make them yourself. In either event, hiring mistakes must be let go. One of my truisms regarding firing a poor employee is this: When faced with the need to terminate an unsatisfactory employee, I remind the other employees that every day we keep a poor employee on the payroll, we are jeopardizing everyone else's jobs. We must focus on the many as well as the one, and then we make sure that we treat the terminated employee fairly.

On-the-Job Training

Training starts the minute the employees walk in the door the first day and is ongoing for their entire career with the bank. We don't have a formal training program, but we have institutionalized an on-the-job training plan based on mentoring, coaching, and rotation. This allows us to continue our high level of customer service in case of absenteeism or vacations. The person responsible for training people in the organization is the supervisor. When hiring, hire someone who can also train; the ability to train should be one of the criteria. Then, coach bosses on how to train to build skills because the best trainer is the boss.

At Embassy, employees learn all parts of the business. If they are a personal banker, we rotate them to all our branches. As of this writing, there are seven branches throughout Lehigh Valley, Pennsylvania, with plans for more. Our total assets are approximately three-quarter of a billion dollars.

When an employee starts, a seasoned employee takes him or her around and introduces him or her to all the different people at the banks, both in customer-facing roles and the back-office support staff. They meet people in commercial lending and consumer lending. Employees make them feel welcome. Then, they are introduced at the monthly staff meeting.

As president and CEO, David Lobach is at the staff meeting, but other people often run it, depending on the topic of the month. Everyone is welcome to present and discuss—everyone from commercial lending, consumer lending, branch management, and the back office. Our commercial-lending people preview what they do. Our back-office operations shares with everybody what they do. In this way, all the employees understand how well the bank is doing, and everyone knows what they are doing is important enough to be a topic for discussion at the monthly meetings. It has impact because they hear those reports from the people in those roles. One of the reasons our customer service is so good out front is that our back office is so good.

David has a unique way of maintaining the focus on the customer and customer satisfaction. He says, "When it comes to the customer, the answer is yes. What is the question?"

His attitude says that we are here to help customers meet their financial goals. No day is easy or unproductive, but it is fun. Yes, it is difficult, but it yields results.

We prefer that promotions come from inside. However, if we lose a highly skilled person and don't have anyone quite ready to take the role, or someone who would like to leave their present role and take it, we hire from the outside. We have a reputation in the local-banking community as a great place to work, and that works in our favor. We lost a vice president of commercial lending and had a waiting list of people from other financial institutions who wanted to come and work for us. We can choose from the best outside our organization when we have to. Our outside hires are passionate about their jobs and are proving their worth every day. Noteworthy is the case of our outside hire for a new vice president of commercial lending because he is doing an outstanding job.

Make It Fun

I learned early in my career that happy employees are productive employees. Back at one of my first roles at

GE, when I took it on myself to pave the parking lot that bothered everyone, people immediately were appreciative. It showed in their attitudes and productivity. I learned then to take care of your people. Embassy Bank is a fun placc to work.

In fact, a number of our employees took the initiative to form a "Culture Club," which plans events for families as well as various activities at the monthly staff meetings to promote teamwork and fun. Staff meetings are anything but dull!

Culture Built around the Customer

The whole success of the bank is built on a customer-focused culture. Some banks have visited Embassy to see how we do what we do. They visit our branches to see if we are offering certain kinds of services that attract customers and keep them happy. But they can't find the answer in our departments and services. The answer to our success is the culture of the bank. David Lobach has developed and maintained the culture, and it's all about the culture. Excellence starts at the top.

Our employees all appreciate and enjoy being part of a community bank, so much so, in fact, that they developed a Declaration of Independence, which outlines what we commit to doing to earn the right to remain independent.

Embassy Bank's Declaration of Independence

When in the course of business events, it becomes evident for one company to publicly proclaim its intentions to the citizens of the community in which it serves. Therefore, Embassy Bank for the Lehigh Valley wishes to declare that it will earn the right, every day, to build shareholder value by being an independent and self governing entity where customers are first priority.

We hold that all banks are not created equal, their success is defined only to what extent they care for their customer, team members, and the community in which they live and serve. Embassy believes that maintaining an undivided focus on the betterment of these principle factors will result in a successful organization. We believe that, by remaining an independent financial institution, we will maintain a superior level of customer service. Our empowered team members will possess the means to take ownership, allowing them to meet and exceed the customer's needs. By remaining local we can retain the power to make decisions that will benefit our stakeholders directly.

Embassy Bank has become a home to customers who no longer wish to be subject to never-ending change at the hands of multiple mergers. Embassy's Board of Directors, management, and employees hereby publish and declare to the citizens of the Greater Lehigh Valley its solemn intent to earn the right to avoid affiliations with larger, controlling financial institutions. As an entity we understand that this right must be earned, therefore we pledge to do this by:

- Taking no action without first considering the impact on the customer.
- Always being responsive to the market, while offering exceptional value and innovative products built to meet customer's needs.
- Providing the most superior customer service, always caring for our people and our diverse community in the interest of serving them for the long term,
- Recognizing each member's personal talents and contributions to our success while mentoring them on their paths to leadership,
- Consistently serving our community through team and individual involvement.
- Remaining vigilant to the moves of our competition; allowing us to create new products and services that will positively impact the customer.
- Continuing to simplify the process of banking by breaking down barriers and eliminating layers of unnecessary hierarchy.

We, therefore, the Team Members of Embassy Bank for the Lehigh Valley, gathering in the entirety, appealing to common sense for the righteousness of our intentions do, in the name of all who are now employed and who may become employed in the future, who are now invested or who may invest in the future, and who may wish to voluntarily join our cause, under the Embassy Bank name and mission, solemnly publish and declare:

Embassy Bank for the Lehigh Valley is and of Right ought to be an Independent Enterprise. We will earn this right and have no design or intention to be acquired by any other. To maintain this right we dedicate ourselves to the principles of our founders; to have an unusual focus on the customer, to make quality the hallmark of all we do, and to never make a commitment we do not intend to keep. And for the support of this Declaration, with firm conviction that our intention is admirable, we mutually pledge to each other and to the public our diligence, dedication and honor.

Our employees know they are valuable, and they value each other. Each person understands that his or her coworkers are quality people all working to make Embassy a great bank. They know they can talk to any other employees at the bank at any time and don't have to follow an archaic organizational chart. The Embassy Bank organizational chart is very flat. That eliminates backbiting. Everyone knows they are all rowing the boat together in the same direction. Employee gossip and undercutting coworkers is at a minimum, if it exists at all. They are focused on performing well and pleasing the customer. Employees are empowered and know that they have the responsibility, authority, and skills for the environment in which they work.

Part of pleasing the customer is making sure that our branches reflect the neighborhoods in which they are located. An outsider might make an assumption about the Lehigh Valley and take the same approach to all the branches. But we understand our community, so we don't take the cookie-cutter approach to our branches. Each branch manager has an individual marketing budget to spend in the way that meets the needs of the community that branch serves.

A suburban branch is very different than an urban branch. What works at a suburban branch isn't necessarily going to work at an urban location and vice versa, so we give them all the free rein. The branch managers feel good about it. They are empowered, and they are the president of Embassy Bank to their customers. Empowering our branch managers is one key to employee satisfaction.

Embassy also structures its accounting and compensation plan to encourage cooperation, not competition, among the branches. At most other banks, branches are normally profit centers. That mentality leads to competition among branches over which branch gets credit for a loan, for example, rather than competing with other banks for the customers' business. At Embassy, our branches are cost centers, not profit centers. It changes the incentives for the people working at the branches and makes people work together for the good of the whole.

For example, if a customer goes to one of our branches and the loan officer takes his loan application for two-hundred-thousand dollars, but the customer signs the loan at another branch because it is more convenient, the branch that originated the loan gets credit for it. Under most other bank branch arrangements, the branch where the loan was signed would take credit for that loan. That causes competition between two branches, and the bank incurs opportunity costs (the cost of opportunities lost due to internal competition). Just as important, shareholders only measure total bank performance, not individual branch performance.

The customer focus is not just management talk. Embassy employees have signed loan documents on a Sunday when our bank is closed if a customer needed it then. An employee delivered bank giveaway gifts to a customer who wanted to use them for party favors. Those kinds of actions tell your customers that you are running a business to satisfy them. The focus has to be on the customers, and it can't just be a motto. You need to back it up with behavior.

The other part of a customer focus is to have simple, easily understood systems so you can deliver on promises to your customers. Make it uncomplicated for your employees to serve their customers well.

Keeping the Culture: Succession Planning

As I found out a number of times in my career, tearing down a culture is easy. Building a culture is hard work, and maintaining that culture takes thought and dedication to the core U-Turn Leadership principles.

At Embassy Bank, a number of people in the organization could be candidates to replace Dave Lobach. The person who replaces David will come from within the bank. Some of them are quite young, but that is in keeping with David's retirement time line. However, if something derails that succession plan, there is a disaster plan. Like any well-run organization, Embassy has a backup plan in place. Because of the bank's great reputation among banking professionals, Embassy is able to hire well.

As I mentioned earlier, people tend to relax when things go well. It is the job of the CEO or the president to always find something to challenge them. David is outstanding at finding new challenges for his employees. He has helped develop people who have benefitted from his leadership and grew in ways that would not have been possible in a more traditional banking culture. He understands their strengths and their weaknesses, and he finds a way to minimize the impact of their weaknesses on how well they do their job.

David has made a lot of people better. He doesn't hire consultants to do it. It is his leadership style, and it is his job to do it! He owns that responsibility.

The bank utilizes a personal-banker position that replaces the traditional teller, as previously mentioned. The personal bankers are trained in all the functions of a traditional teller but with a much broader customer focus so that they can satisfy customers and, if necessary, redirect them. With their knowledge of the entire bank operation, they are much better equipped to answer preliminary questions for customers. They don't have to refer customers to another employee in another function or another location to answer questions. They also have loan authority.

We also have a very flat organization. If consultants were to look at our organization, they would say we have matrix management. For example, because our personal bankers have loan authority, in addition to working for the branch manager, they also work for the consumer-lending officer. It works great. We don't make a big deal of these differences from the traditional banking model; we just do it!

We also have no silos. Horizontal communication is excellent. Today's information and communication technology enables this informal relationship structure to facilitate cross-functional communication.

As I discussed in the last chapter, Embassy does not create static job descriptions. The bank creates statements of expectations that look to the future and to where the

Elmer D. Gates

business is going. We don't have job descriptions that describe where it was and how we are going to keep it that way. Today, with the pace of change, a static job description would be foolish.

Statements of expectation look toward the future and can be very short term. In fact, they may not be written because of the way technology is changing and made possible due to the mutual trust that exists throughout the bank. What we want to do today might be totally different from what we want to do next year due to what new technology makes possible. Banking is going through the technological revolution as much as any other industry. We also are being bombarded by new regulations, most unnecessary and written by people with no banking experience. This confluence of changes means we want to stay flexible to respond to external factors.

Recently, there was an article on banking in the local newspaper asking, "Would you rather stand in line or go online to do your banking?" Banking has to adjust to that. At Embassy, we are.

Beyond the Bank: Mentoring

In recent years, I've been mentoring owners of both established companies and start-up companies using the U-Turn Leadership principles I've learned throughout my career.

One notable turnaround was a company led by a distressed socialite whose father had died leaving her with a trust fund and his business. She became the CEO. After a few years, the business started losing money. A friend asked me to get involved, so I volunteered to help her. The business produced an excellent product that was well-accepted in their industry; they were a custom sheet-metal fabrication shop.

When we first met, her trust fund had just run out. She had been using the proceeds of the trust fund to make up for losses in the business. She had always lived well and was desperate. She was planning to lay off a salesman.

It was clear that her strong suit was not business acumen. I agreed to help her straighten out her business, but first, I established a few rules.

"Tell me how much you can live on. Give me a monthly number," I said.

She gave me her number.

"You can take that much out of the business each month and no more. That is the condition for my getting involved." She agreed and kept her agreement.

I asked to see her operating statement. In twenty minutes, I found her problem. She was selling her product below cost. She didn't need to lower her costs; she had a great product. She needed to raise her prices. I convinced her to raise her prices. Her customers accepted it without a single complaint.

Within three months, she was breaking even. Within six months, she was making money at an annual profit rate of one-hundred-thousand dollars with a plan to grow the business substantially. The business continued to grow, and soon she was minting money. She decided she didn't need me anymore but was afraid to tell me.

I laughed and said, "If you fire me, I'll be ahead." I left, and we remained friends.

I have always mentored business people at no cost. It is a pleasure for me, and if they don't like the result, they can't complain about the price!

⁝

I find much of what I learned from successes in fixing companies is very helpful in mentoring start-ups as well. The main difference between fixing a failing business and organizing a startup is that I am using the lessons learned to prevent mistakes rather than fix them. Frankly, this is even more rewarding than fixing failed businesses.

First, you need to ask yourself why you are in business. What are you trying to do? Hint: the right answer is "to get rich." Next, ask yourself: what are going to be the elements of success of this business compared to our competition?

In the case of Embassy Bank, those answers were that we were going to run lean, have a very flexible workforce, have a culture where people want to be a part of it, do whatever it takes to satisfy a customer and make good profits on a sustained basis, and satisfy our shareholders.

Those same activities, when applied at a start-up, can put the organization on solid footing from the outset. The four keys to successful start-ups include the following:

1. Focus on profit making.
2. Manage cash flow.
3. Don't give away enhancements; charge for them.
4. Assess skills needed and hire skills complementary to your own.

How to Approach Structure and Cash Flow as a Start-up

I started mentoring Matt Bieber Jr., a student at Lehigh University in Bethlehem, Pennsylvania, when he was a college sophomore.

He told me, "Mr. Gates, I can't wait to get out of here and start making money."

I told his parents, "He'll be a millionaire by the time he is thirty." And he is.

I walked the road with him. He developed a company and had a partner working on a system for high-speed trading on Wall Street, where a millisecond means millions of dollars.

He came to me about how to structure the company. "Mr. Gates, we need to understand who is going to be the CEO and who is going to be the COO."

I asked him, "Did you go into business to make money or to have a title?"

"To make money," he said.

"Then what difference does it make what your title is? You are the creative one, so why don't you just put on your business card, *The Creative Guy*? And the other guy is the solutions guy, so his card can say *The Solutions Guy*," I suggested.

That is the kind of thinking that start-ups need to engage in. The day of the CEO title may be numbered. We have to start having some creativity in how we organize companies and how we label employees. New information and communication technologies present an opportunity to utilize new organization concepts. We can de-layer organizations. The organization chart used universally today was designed one hundred years ago in an era when we didn't even have telephones.

I suggested to him, "In your company, you might consider having a series of solution centers that are totally interconnected so that horizontal communication can be facilitated."

People running start-ups need to be focused on achieving objectives, not worried about titles. If the business is successful and grows, focus on structure becomes very important as you hire individuals with complementary skills. A business needs structure, not bureaucracy; it is a fine line that divides the two.

One reason entrepreneurs fail is that they run out of cash because they are so busy focusing on their baby. While blindly pursing their passion, entrepreneurs will tend to keep improving their product. In the process, they'll give the improvements away rather than charge customers for it. Soon, they are out of cash because they are focusing on product development and forgetting about where their cash is coming from. Remember, we said businesses can fail with too much emphasis on one aspect of the business at the expense of the others.

To further discuss the high-speed trading entrepreneur, when he was developing the high-speed training programs, he loved the new technology involved. Meanwhile, he had built a software-service business that was generating a consistent and reliable cash flow.

He told me, "I am going to get rid of it. Software service is a boring part of business."

"Let's examine that for a minute. Where are you getting all the cash that allows you to do all this fancy high-speed, high-tech stuff?" I asked him.

"I am getting that from the software-service business," he responded.

I looked at him in the eyes and said nothing needs to be sold. "Find somebody who likes the software-service business and let him or her run it, but don't sell it. You bill your customers at the end of the month and get paid in thirty days. That's good cash flow. That will keep you going. That will give you the money to go out and do all the fancy stuff you are doing."

He was going to get rid of it, and fortunately he didn't.

While another company beat him to market with the trading software, he soon found other applications and continues increasing his wealth to this day.

Another local entrepreneur who developed a very successful global technology business made it a practice to personally sign every check that went out of his business until he left the business. He knew where every penny went. It was his way of keeping tabs on what was happening. The lesson: make sure you pay attention to the details of any business.

Business school teaches start-ups to develop a business plan that contains an exit strategy. In fact, there is an unusual focus on planning and too little on execution. Plans are of little value until they are executed. Schools should put an emphasis on teaching execution. That's as least as hard as planning!

Hiring Practices for Start-ups

Entrepreneurs need to make sure they hire complementary skills. Early-stage entrepreneurs tend to hire people with skill sets like theirs. This is a particularly serious mistake. For example, if they are comfortable with technology, they need to assess the complementary skill sets they need to grow to the next stage and hire those.

Due to the pace of change and technological advancement, entrepreneurs need to think about how to marry technology with business processes. Whether you are running a high-tech company or not, there are some good business practices that cut across all industries:

1. Run lean.
2. Whenever you have an opening, never replace in kind. Do a quick organizational review.
3. Hire complementary skills.
4. Keep a sharp eye on cash.

A Bad Economy Doesn't Affect a Good Idea

Practices employed in a turnaround work in a start-up. In a startup, you are not fixing the business; you are building a culture of success. As you are building a culture of success from the ground up, you have the opportunity to navigate trends that work for you and trends that work against you so you can prevail in both cases.

As I told the congressman, who complained about the effect of the strong dollar on trade, when I was at Fuller, your individual business does not need to be part of the general economy. An individual business, run well and with great thought, energy, and customer focus, can thrive in any business environment.

David Lobach and I founded Embassy Bank in the early 2000s as the United States and global economy began its downward spiral. Because David said, "We will not participate in the recession," Embassy Bank is a living testament to the fact that it is possible.

In the next and final chapter, we will look at the inverse of that philosophy. We will look at a huge global corporation that crashed and failed while its industry and the global economy thrived. As you will see, Bethlehem Steel proved the point that an individual business can decide its own fate and whether or not it will participate in the prevailing economic conditions.

Chapter 9: Takeaways

1. Hire for attitude; train for aptitude.
2. Delegate responsibility and hold individuals accountable for results.
3. Look for actions that go above and beyond and celebrate them.
4. Run lean.
5. Give meaning to every employee's work by empowering each one.
6. Success is hard work. Don't let up.
7. Defy convention in all aspects of the business.
8. Keep finding new challenges.
9. Keep an eye on your cash flow.
10. Hire skills complementary to your own.

Elmer D. Gates

Chapter 10

Echoes from the Lost:
The Story of Bethlehem Steel

The toughest business to run is a successful one. Everyone wants to relax.

Sometimes it's too late.

A business rarely ever goes from healthy to unhealthy in a short period of time. Most often, there is a series of small and seemingly insignificant negative actions or inactions, which, in the judgment of management, do not require remedial action. A series of such events over time will ultimately create the need for a turnaround. Businesses in this situation can be at any stage of development, from early-stage to mature companies.

In the case of Bethlehem Steel Corporation, it was not just another mature company that was in failure. It was a global corporation that provided the steel that built the battleships of WWI and WWII, the I-beams that provided the erector-set structure of the Empire State Building, and the bright-orange steel that bedecks the Golden Gate Bridge.

What happened? My being in Bethlehem during the period of decline gifted me with an informed opinion, one that I'm sure to this day will irk some people who will read this. I have never allowed the worry of what other people think affect my public opinion. This is my view of reality, but it is not an outlier view. It is one that aligns with other informed opinions from those who also had an insider's perspective, including the late, great Pulitzer Prize-winning editor of the now-defunct Bethlehem Globe-Times, John Strohmeyer, who wrote a clear-eyed, unapologetic analysis in 1986, *Crisis in Bethlehem*.[6]

⣿

To analyze the demise of Bethlehem Steel, let's start by reviewing principles we discussed earlier. In examining a business failure, one or several of the following conditions exist:

- inept, distracted or uninvolved leadership
- an internal focus
- a culture of comfort and satisfaction
- failure to control costs
- a lack of focus on new competition in the global market
- a failure to seriously consider technological innovation by global competitors

---

[6] Strohmeyer, John. *Crisis in Bethlehem*. Maryland: Adler & Adler, 1986.

At Bethlehem Steel, one or more of these critical elements of business failure were in play at all times. Sometimes, to try to stop the bleeding, executives put an unusual focus on solving a single element at the expense of all the others.

Make no mistake. A quick rotation of CEOs in the last decades of the company's life demonstrated that the board of directors tried to wrest victory from the jaws of defeat. I knew the last CEOs and had discussions with each of them at different lengths and levels of detail. No matter the rescue tactics they implemented, ultimately those tactics were reactive, poorly employed, and did not unseat the culture of comfort that had embedded itself in the fabric of the Bethlehem Steel Company.

Protecting the Status Quo

A once great and respected company, a world leader in its industry, arrived at the point of no return through a series of compromises, poor decisions, and a default culture of complacency. Unfortunately, the board of directors and the executive leadership team recognized too late that it needed a major fix, and they failed to save the company.

In World War II, Allied forces destroyed all the steelmaking capacity in the world. For a decade after the war, Germany and Japan had no steel industry. During that time, in the heady years following the Allied victory, American steelmakers had a global monopoly. They felt invincible in every way. In a monopoly of any sort, you have unlimited freedom to charge the customers what is needed to cover your costs.

In the aftermath of WWII, the United States gave a hand up to its war-ravaged rivals. The US Secretary of State and former General of the Army Joint Chiefs of Staff, George C. Marshall, developed and implemented The Marshall Plan to restore the economies of our former enemies. The Marshall Plan helped Germany and Japan rebuild their steelmaking capacity.

During this postwar era, the world's scientific and industrial minds experienced a heightened interest in innovation, research, and entrepreneurship. As a result, global technical innovation flourished. The French developed a continuous-casting steel manufacturing process, which improved productivity and reduced the cost of steelmaking. American innovation gave birth to mini mills that used scrap steel, eliminating the need and cost to process ore.

The benevolent Marshall Plan, combined with the new steelmaking technologies, helped Germany and Japan rebuild their steel capacity in ways that surpassed their former American rivals. The newly built steel plants were more modern and productive than much of the capacity in the United States. After a few years of basking in the postwar monopolistic environment, Bethlehem Steel found itself in significant competition with its more modern German and Japanese counterparts. Bethlehem was forced to compete with the new entrants while bearing the direct and indirect costs of actions taken during its monopolistic era. Bethlehem Steel struggled in this global competition.

Meanwhile, a comfortable Bethlehem Steel culture continued to enjoy the status quo. The company still relied on processing iron ore and used a slightly refined Bessemer converter technology developed in 1855. It was a hot, dangerous, costly, labor- and natural-resource-intensive process. But because the company was a global force for most of the mid-twentieth century, its leadership did not understand that it was not invincible. While Bethlehem Steel rested on past glory, its competitors had modernized so that the quality of their products was equal or superior, and their prices were less. By the time Bethlehem Steel executives looked up from their golf carts and finely manicured lawns, it was too late.

A Culture of Comfort

Most notably, employees of "the Steel" wore an air of superiority. That attitude was buttressed by a small town that relied on its wealthy corporate patron. When the City of Bethlehem needed a new town hall, Bethlehem Steel paid its taxes two or three years ahead of time in order to finance construction. With that kind of clout, its executives wielded a lot of power throughout the community.

The ensconced Bethlehem executive contingent didn't worry about competition; they didn't worry about technological change. They were living in a false environment. In a word, they just got sloppy.

While French, German, and Japanese competitors produced low-cost, quality steel, Bethlehem Steel executives enjoyed the perks of power, position, and prestige in a small town. The company executives had access to limousines and private planes housed at a private corporate hangar at the regional airport. People who were sweeping the floors made eighteen dollars per hour back in the 1980s, when minimum wage was little more than three dollars per hour.

In acts of stunning largesse, the board voted to build a private and exclusive golf course for the use of executives and non-Steel local members of Saucon Valley Country Club and guests. Saucon Valley Country Club features one of the country's best golf courses, built and maintained at considerable expense. The company also feted middle management with a golf club of its own. Executives had their spacious lawns manicured and substantial homes repaired at company expense. Lest the steelworkers down in the fiery furnaces be forgotten, the United Steelworkers of America negotiated 13 weeks' vacation every five years for its long-time members.

Bethlehem Steel Company just forgot how to run a company because it was easier to raise prices than it was to get another point or two of productivity. That kind of short-term thinking has a short life span.

Strohmeyer's book examines, in searing detail, executive decisions that protected the insular culture in

Bethlehem from attempts to expand beyond its parochial footprint and mind-set. I won't recount those decisions here, but I highly recommend Strohmeyer's book as essential U-Turn Leadership reading that describes the downward spiral of a global industrial giant. It's a veritable "how-not-to" of lean leadership.

Forward Guard

When I first arrived in Bethlehem, I met an executive of one of the larger regional banks. He was a vibrant and energetic leader in the community. As I became active in the community from my position as CEO of The Fuller Company, we saw one of the impacts of Bethlehem Steel's benevolence was that Bethlehem Steel people ran everything in the local nonprofit organizations, such as the Boys and Girls Clubs. Given the increasingly precarious position of the steel company, we said, "We've got to start developing leaders outside Bethlehem Steel."

The regional bank executive and I started Leadership Bethlehem, which has become Leadership Lehigh Valley. It still exists today and is managed by Northampton Community College. Our intention was not necessarily to displace the steel's local power; rather, it was a forward guard-action to put a continuity plan in place for the community when "the Steel" influence ceased to exist.

In one of the true ironies of industrial history, in 1898, an early proponent of applying engineering science processes to management Frederick Winslow Taylor joined Bethlehem Steel as a management consultant to solve an expensive machine-shop capacity problem. Taylor and a team of assistants applied Taylor's scientific management principles to increase mass production. Taylor's principles of scientific management form the basis for much of industrial engineering today, including efficiency and elimination of waste. Taylor particularly emphasized work ethic and was open in his disdain for tradition preserved merely for its own sake or to protect the social status of particular workers with particular skill sets. Taylor is, in fact, the great-granddaddy of the lean movement. A gymnasium on Lehigh University's campus on Bethlehem's south side near the former steel site bears his name.

In a conversation with one of the last CEOs of Bethlehem Steel Company, I suggested that he get more aggressive in his efforts to save the company. I had visited his office; his receptionist's office area was larger than the entire executive suite at Fuller Company.

"I need to lay some people off," he told me.

I said, "Whatever number you come up with, double it and lay that many people off because you are just chasing the curve downward. You've got to get ahead of the curve."

He ignored me. He was head of a three- or four-billion-dollar company, and I was CEO of a quarter-billion-dollar company. I am sure he thought, "What does this guy know? He's not a nationally known executive like I am."

Unfortunately, the turnaround effort started too late. Bethlehem Steel stands as a study in pride and greed—a sad footnote in America's industrial history.

As for Bethlehem Steel's role in industrial history, I was told about the plans for a National Museum of Industrial History on the site of the former steel plant. I was invited and sat on the board with some local contractors and other people who stood to benefit from it. Finally, I quit when I saw millions of dollars in donations being spent, with no clear progress on the museum.

I said, "If you build that museum, I am going to build a museum that shows how greed caused a once-great company to fail."

In the end, I didn't build a museum. I wrote a book.

Chapter 10: Takeaways

1. If you run your business like you're in a turnaround situation, you'll never be in a turnaround situation.
2. Never get comfortable. The CEO has the responsibility for this.
3. Continuously measure elements of the environment that impact your business (technology, markets, and competition).
4. Culture starts at the top. Don't delegate this responsibility.
5. Reject the status quo.

Appendices

Think Like a CEO

Random Thought Provokers

- Trust your intuition (your gut!). It's the summation of your life's experiences.
- By failing to make a decision, you really are making a decision not to act.
- Make errors of commission, not omission. If your decision is a bad one, make a new one to correct it.
- If you wait until you have all the facts, the opportunity probably has been lost.
- Leaders are decisive.
- Apologize. Don't ask!
- Every mistake is tuition. Learn from it!
- Leaders do the right thing; managers do things right. Leaders use management processes to get things done.
- Leaders are paid to think. Identify where and when you do your best thinking! Make thinking a habit.
- A leader is never satisfied. Today's accomplishment is the foundation for tomorrow's improvement.
- Negative attitudes are cancerous in an organization. Fix them and fire them!
- Apathy is the enemy of excellence.
- Excellence is a journey, not a destination.
- Listen and silent are spelled with the same letters; open, honest, two-way communication requires listening as well as talking.

- The toughest business to run is a successful one. A leader's job is to keep challenging the organization.
- Structure is required in an organization; bureaucracy is not!
- Always run lean—it's a great way to prioritize work.
- The best way to avoid a layoff is not to hire in the first place.
- Great people will not let the enterprise fail.
- Minimize layers in an organization. Each layer slows decision-making and filters communication.
- Always ask, "Will this add value to the enterprise?" Think two or three times before adding a report. Time spent reporting takes time away from thinking or executing.
- Plans are necessary, but without execution, they are worthless. Focus on execution; spend as much time on execution as on planning.
- The boss is the last one to know that an employee is not performing!
  - First to know: the employee
  - Next to know: his or her fellow workers
  - Last to know: the boss
- There is a time to save money and a time to spend money. Know the difference!
- High expectations are the basis for a high-performing organization.
- Leaders are courageous.
- Leaders make sacrifices!

- time
- health
- friends
- family
- Leaders coach on the spot.
- Leaders constantly measure the external environment.
- Leaders lead by example. Make sure it is the right example.
- Leaders improve the performance of individuals reporting to them and improve every process for which he or she is responsible.
- Sole proprietors perform every function in the business—buying, selling, costing, pricing, and advertising. Act like a sole proprietor.
- Adding costs is much easier than reducing costs. ("It is easier to build costs in than to take them out.")
- Never replace open positions in kind. Use the opportunity to look at the division of work as well as the technology and the skill sets of remaining employees.
- The opposite of success is failure. Succeeding is hard. Failing is easy. Go for success!

Blue-Collar Leadership Lessons

The job of a leader is to get results.

- It is not "to follow the process."
- You may use the process to get the results.
- Too many CEOs "play the role."
- Leaders do the right thing; managers do things right.

The most important attribute of leadership is integrity:

- integrity of communication—face-to-face, in writing, and in actions
- integrity in treatment of everyone
- integrity in decision-making
- integrity in negotiating results to be achieved, meaning two-way

My formula for success includes:

- unusual focus on the customer;
- quality in all you do;
- answering the phone/letters;
- good treatment of everyone; and
- never making a commitment you don't intend to keep.

You achieve results with your leadership style.

- It is unique and personal.
- There is no "one size fits all" leadership style.
- Your leadership style is shaped by your ethnicity, gender, upbringing, education, and experience.
- Do not read leadership books or articles on how to lead in order to imitate them; read them to find which attributes successful leaders have embraced.
- Don't copy any leaders' styles; refine your own.

Always run lean. Great people won't let the enterprise fail. Each of us is capable of more.

Never replace "in kind."

- Replacing "in kind" is hiring for the past.
- Every opening is an opportunity.
  - Study the division of work.
  - Assess the impact of technology.
  - Reassign people to match talent with need.
- The preceding results in hiring for the future.

Attributes of Leaders

- never satisfied, which does not mean dissatisfied
- consistent
- available
- judges each event on its own merit
- accepts failure, if failure results from the effort to improve
- earns trust, which can't be bestowed
- takes risks
- makes sacrifices
- good listener
- consistent
- decisive
- looks ahead, not back

Leadership Isn't

- popularity;
- personality;
- names on an organizational chart;
- watching things happen; or
- taking credit.

Signs of a Leaderless Organization

- inward focus (don't know customers or customers are an intrusion)
- lack of excitement and energy
- focus on self
- no accountability
- lack of fun
- lack of creativity and innovation

Building an Entrepreneurial Culture
Five Steps for Entrepreneurs

1. Understand principles of leadership and leadership style.
2. Negotiate job responsibilities to give employees ownership.
3. Empower yourself and your employees.
4. Improve the organization every day.
5. Create an organization of entrepreneurs.

Tips for Hopeful Entrepreneurs

1. You can be entrepreneurial in a big organization.
   - Look at yourself as the CEO of your responsibilities.
   - Take ownership of your responsibilities.

- Empower yourself to lead your area of responsibility.
- Recognize you have suppliers and customers and treat them well.
- Learn all the details of your responsibilities.
- Improve your part of the business every day and treat it as your own company.

Did you do those things? Now you are an entrepreneur in a large organization!

2. If you plan to start a business, it will take twice as long and cost twice as much as your forecast. Plan that way!

3. No leader is on the organizational chart.
   - Coffee machine leaders: beware of them and make sure they are on your side.
   - Leaders in the time of emergencies: we call them heroes.

4. Leaders have the responsibility to improve the performance of all the people reporting to them and to improve every process for which they are responsible.

5. Use lessons from coaches of athletic teams to improve people's performance.

- Coach people, don't appraise them. Coaching is positive, while appraising is negative.
- Open, honest, two-way communication is critical in coaching people.
- Coach on the spot.
- Use the 4-x-100 rule: 100 percent honest 100 percent of the time with 100 percent of your people in 100 percent of their coaching sessions.

6. The leader is responsible for building and maintaining the culture of the organization.
   - Every organization has a culture, either by default or decision. Make sure yours is based on decisions.
   - Building and maintaining a culture is very hard work, and it is the job of the leaders. It cannot be delegated.
   - Great cultures can be destroyed in a very short period of time.

7. Leaders are paid to think, not do.
   - Doing is easy; thinking is hard.
   - Make time to think.
   - Make others think. Build a thinking organization.

About the Author

Elmer D. Gates grew up in modest circumstances in a rural Adirondack Mountain area of New York state. He graduated from Clarkson University in 1950 with a degree in mechanical engineering. During the Korean War, he served as a combat engineering platoon leader, spending his final year of service in a series of army hospitals. He was married for fifty-five years to his wife, Betty, who was a tremendous support to his career. She passed away in 2008. Elmer has two daughters, Patti Smith and Jodi Key, and four grandchildren. He credits Clarkson for preparing him for a successful and rewarding career, much of it with General Electric.

After leaving General Electric in 1982, his entrepreneurial spirit led him to enter the "turnaround business." He led an LBO of Fuller Company in 1986 and, as president and CEO, took it to a global leadership position in 1990, when he sold it to its most formidable competitor. He has since been a mentor to many, from start-up entrepreneurs to CEOs of significant importance, including not-for-profit organizations.

Elmer describes his life as "well-lived." He was honored with the Clarkson Golden Knight Award in 2010 and inducted into Clarkson's Alumni Entrepreneurial Hall of Fame in 2011. In 2012, he was inducted into the Lehigh Valley Executive Hall of Fame.

Index

C

organizational chart 121, 173, 204, 206
organizational structure 86, 122
overhead expense 123
overtime 36, 39, 41, 42, 44, 45
ownership 45, 73, 75, 76, 78, 97, 143, 205
ownership mentality 143

P

Pakistan 89, 107, 108, 131
Paris 100
parts shortage 36, 37, 45
patent applications 146
pay rate 48
Pennsylvania 28, 66, 80, 82, 99, 107, 128, 161, 169, 180
Pennsylvania Dutch culture 99
performance appraisals 141, 142, 143
performance-based contract 60
personal attributes 71
personal bankers 163, 164, 169, 176
personality 32, 86, 92, 125, 167, 204
personality tests 167
pickets 33, 34, 35
Pittsfield, Massachusetts 59
pleasing the customer 173
political environment 94
poor leadership 53
poor productivity 88
position description 29, 30, 140
price 46, 47, 55, 104, 122, 148, 155, 178, 179, 191, 192

price increase 104
printed circuit boards 18
product development 146, 182
production control manager 23, 24
production runs 35
productive employees 170
professional development 28, 73
profitability xiv, 45, 51, 123, 124
profit centers 173, 174
profit making 180
project manager 25, 26, 99, 102, 103, 111
project review 89, 102, 103
promotions 12, 48, 53, 170
purchasing 37, 46, 95, 148

Q

Quality xv, xvi, 5, 31, 36, 37, 38, 41, 43, 44, 45, 48, 61, 62, 67, 85, 88, 89, 120, 129, 131, 149, 155, 172, 191, 192, 202
quality control 37, 41

R

RCA 32
recession 165, 184
relationships 5, 73, 75, 86, 88, 108, 119, 120, 121, 122, 134, 138, 149, 150, 151, 152, 153, 162, 163, 164, 176
relationship strategy 134, 149, 150, 151, 163
remedial action 81, 187
respect xvii, 25, 58, 67, 68, 74, 93, 113, 120, 121, 134, 135
revenue projection 103